MW01632930

Writing Our Lives

A Southern Storytellers Anthology

Writing Our Lives

A Southern Storytellers Anthology

INTRODUCING

Darneisha F. Airhart, Ricky Allen, Marla Cantrell, Jill Cox-Cordova, Tanja Enoch, Angela Griffith-Newkirk, Byron Hodges, Phyllis Hodges, Janet Holmes Uchendu, Felix Kariuki, Janetta Kearney, Renee ' La Viness, Jonelle Grace Lipscomb, Angel Morgan, Paula Releford, JoSephine Rumph, and Teddy Warria

Writing our World Publishing, LLC
and Butterfly Publishing,

First Writing Our World Press Edition Volume V 2021

Printed in the United States of America

ISBN 978-0-9889644-9-5 (paperback)
ISBN 978-0-692-09921-6 (ebook)

Editing, Jill Cox-Cordova
Interior Design, WOW! Publishing
Cover Design, Kenosis Design Innovations

Writing Our World Publishing
2 Rosier Court,
Little Rock, Arkansas 72211

To the brave southern writers
who keep making our world better
by sharing their joys and pain.

Foreword

Writing our Lives and our Changing World.

I'm thinking of the iconic photograph of the beautiful, lone flower that miraculously blooms in the crack of a concrete sidewalk. Thriving, not merely surviving. Someone had the insight to document that miracle of nature.

That is what we do when we write and share our stories, whether they're about the good, the bad or the miraculous—each serves as a link to our world. Take the health pandemic that gripped our world in March 2020, a health scourge so horrific it left no corner of the world untouched. We all read the stories and heard the news reports of COVID's horrific impact on families and children around the world. But, what of our own personal experiences? How were our personal lives, our families and communities changed?

Imagine: Your story may be the very one that answers the questions for the next generation who will surely ask the hard questions about our world, some 100 years from now. While we are taught that we write for ourselves first and foremost, I pray that some of us feel the charge to write for others, to help ensure a better tomorrow. I've been thinking a lot about what this harsh season has meant for writers and other creatives. I applaud those who found a way to survive and thrive despite it all. I celebrate those who found ways to make stories part of the solution—elevating stories of our past, using them as bridges to our future.

We hope you will celebrate our five years of being a part of the literary community by taking time to read this Fifth Anniversary Edition of the Southern Anthology. While each story speaks to our writers' personal experiences, they also speak to our world today and yesterday. The power of stories is inarguable. They teach us about ourselves and our world. Stories make us better and make us know our worth. The strength of our world and our people, is in how we value and remember our stories.

Janis F. Kearney writer, publisher, journalist, and writing instructor, cofounded Read.Write.Share Writers Weekend in 2015, with Iris M. Williams, founder of Butterfly Publishing Company. She purchased the historic Arkansas State Press Newspaper from Civil Rights legend Daisy Gatson Bates in 1988 and was appointed as the first-ever Personal Presidential Diarist tasked with chronicling the presidency of William J. Clinton.

Janis founded Writing our World Publishing, a micro-publishing company in 2003. She was selected as a fellow at the Harvard University W.E.B. DuBois Institute of African and African American Studies, as a Humanities Fellow at Chicago's DePaul University, and as a Visiting Humanities Scholar and Professor at Arkansas State University, Jonesboro. She was awarded the Lemke Journalism Award from her Alma Mater, University of Arkansas, and into the Arkansas Writers Hall of Fame in 2016. She has authored and co-authored 15 books. The second in her murder mystery imprint, Cajun Lawmen Murder Mysteries, is scheduled to debut January 2022, and her biography *Mahalia: Orphan Queen*, is scheduled for publication October 2022.

Janis founded the Celebrate! Maya Project of Arkansas, following the death of literary icon Maya Angelou. The project seeks to increase the awareness of Angelou's life and legacy throughout the state and help youth realize their academic and artistic dreams through workshops and academic scholarships and poetry awards.
https://www.wowpublishing.org
https://www.rwsweekend.org
https://celebratemayaproject.org

Iris M. Williams author, publisher, speaker, and writing coach, cofounded **Read.Write.Share Writers Weekend** in 2015, with Janis. F. Kearney, founder of Writing our World Publishing.

As Proprietor and Managing Editor of **Butterfly Typeface Publishing,** Iris M. Williams has labored extensively since the company's launch in 2014 to provide quality publishing services at affordable prices.

Also, an author, *An Abundant Life, Faith in Self,* Iris understands the emotional and financial burdens of self-publishing and is determined to approach her publishing business from the perspective of the author.

To this end, she diligently reviews each manuscript and lends her years of experience in hopes of making good great!

A lifelong learner, Iris is also an educator. She coaches authors in their craft with workshops and has also taught *The Basics of Publishing and Memoir Writing* for National Park College in Hot Springs, Arkansas.

Iris currently resides in Little Rock, Arkansas, loves reading, listening to music, writing stories, and helping others find their voice.

To learn more about the author and publisher, visit:
www.irismwilliams.com

www.butterflyflytypeface.com

Here Come the Cousins

BY DARNEISHA F. AIRHART

The invisible choir of "kay-dee-deeds" (cicadas) loudly sing. The hazy sunshine slowly sets and me and Pawpaw are porch sittin'. Every so often my granny would gently open the screen door and peek her head out, the dish towel flung across her shoulder, and repeat what she had just said fifteen minutes prior.

"Hun, it's getting late, don't you think they should have been here by now?" she'd ask Pawpaw.

And like a script from a movie, he would repeat his line, "Well, they probably had tuh make a few stops, Hun."

Granny would nod in agreement and turn around, heading back inside to the kitchen where she was preparing for the big arrival with a big ol' pot of somethin' on the stove, smellin' good, along with my favorite: her skillet cornbread.

My eight-year-old self was excited. Yet, unable to understand all the emotions goin' on inside myself, I did realize I was feelin' a bit of non-excitement, too.

It always seemed to be a Thursday evening, not quite the weekend, (also during the hottest part of July), same day, same time every year that the Big Time Kansas City Family Vacation to Arkansas took place.

Yes, I could feel it all week before they came. Granny would have me helping her change

bedsheets and all sorts of extra grocery store visits (which were fun). There was also the purchase of lots of new cereals that I didn't eat on a regular basis, like Alpha Bits (which I never really liked anyway).

It was beginning to get dusk, and I knew Granny would return shortly to ask Pawpaw the same question again, so I decided to go stand in the yard. I left my white strappy sandals scooted underneath the metal lawn chair I'd been seated in when I chatted with Pawpaw, swatting flies with the long-handled swatter. The shimmery rainbow of beads on each neatly-twined cornrow braid dangled against my paper-sack brown, chubby little cheeks. It made a click clack as I jumped down the steps one by one and stood in my spot in the freshly-cut grass, next to the round red bush (my lookout spot as if I were an army scout or something). I peered up past the Valley Foods grocery store that sat about a block from our house.

After standing there for what seemed like only a few seconds, I could see that long yet strange-looking vehicle turning the corner onto our street. I called out, "Pawpaw! Granny! Here they come."

The closer they got, we all began waving, and finally, they were here pulling right up into the gravel driveway. The windows on every side of Uncle's car were rolled down, each with two or three heads poking out and hands flailing wildly about, so I saw the noticeable aha moment on each face. I even heard someone say, "Ooh, look at Granddaddy's house."

That was because last summer the front porch was steel gray, and the wood-framed home was bright white. Granny and Pawpaw's house was now yellow with a dusty brown trim, sorta like chocolate icing with not enough chocolate. So, everyone was a bit giddy over how nice Pawpaw's choice of paint color had actually turned out, even though it was not Granny's favorite. But she generally let Pawpaw handle those outdoor things, just as long as it didn't interfere with her vibrant gladiolas and hydrangeas she was joyfully known around the neighborhood for growing.

When my seven cousins, uncle, and aunty slowly stepped out of their fancy LTD 1975 station wagon, the tight hugs, cheek kisses, and big laughs began.

"Ooh, we glad y'all made it safely. Come on in this house and get y'all somethin' tuh eat," Granny said as she hugged her son, my great uncle, tightly along with a few heavy pats on his back.

Pawpaw stood up from his favorite seat on the porch. He was wearing his comfy but neatly ironed khaki's, a short-sleeved white button up, and, of course, his brown outdoor slippers me and mama had gotten him for Christmas.

Stepping onto the sidewalk he had paved some 15 years prior, with his low snow-white hair against handsome ebony skin and a shiny natural smile, he leaned into give Aunty O, a good hug. "You don't age a bit," he said.

All Granny wanted everyone to do, in that moment, was go have a bite to eat, which she alluded to several times sayin' things like, "I know y'all must be hungry . . . go fix them kids a plate."

I was the youngest person on the scene, and I was kinda just standing back observing all the lovely, boisterous chatter and engagement. My dainty hands gripped her blue and white gingham shift, which blew whatever way the summery breeze went, sending a hint of Charlie perfume from her Avon collection, which she would give me a little spritz on my wrist on Sunday mornings for church. She was my beautiful barrier until I decided to participate in all the fanfare.

My uncle and aunty both grinned when I stepped frontward closer to them. They mentioned how "pretty" I was and how I was "gettin' to be such a big girl."

When everyone began meandering away from the car, here come my "city" cousins oohing and ahing over me like an exhibit at the discovery museum saying, "Look at little Neisha. She is getting taller." They would burst into laughter trying to mimic my southern drawl, which was unapparent to me.

"Hi, Cuh-zen," they would say in unison, then grab their bellies in laughter.

Well, I'd smile, but as much as I had been happy about their arrival, within that first fifteen minutes of all the gaieties and joyful faces, I was just as ready for them to leave.

DK was the exception; he was my favorite, my superhero cousin who made sure his siblings treated me nice and that I got goodies when we'd all trek to the corner market or have daily adventures around town, like the city park playground, where he would help me maneuver the giant silver slide and the swings.

Considering all that was taking place, I began to see that it wasn't only that my southern vernacular would be on trial for the next six days, but my summer break and regular routine of things was also about to be put on hold, Yeah, as long as the "guests" were in town, my sitting in the kitchen slurping creamy coffee from a saucer with Granny and giggling over how I'm supposed to cool it before I drank it too hot, watching her cook sweet potato pies, getting to lick the beaters from the mixer once she finished preparing cake batter, holding the water hose and watering the flowers, or sitting out on the front lawn selling watermelons with Pawpaw with me getting to place the dollar bills in the old cigar box, would all be on hold.

With all these folks around and every bed and room in the house filled, there were rollaway beds and pull-out couches all overtaken during summer visits. I'd have to change my reign of Granny and Pawpaw's abode. Until all the visitors returned to their own homes, there would be no playin' music after dinner on Pawpaw's radio (that he only used to listen to baseball games) or playin' dress up in Granny's room or coloring on the back porch at noon.

So, for now, my country fun of receiving first great-grand child attention, like evening drives, going fishin', or just us three watching *Hee Haw,* would have to wait.

Truth be told, I guess my cousins didn't always give me the blues, even though it may have seemed to be the case. They were fun at times and not all the love was lost, but I was still pretty certain that the Midwest had invaded the South.

Darneisha F. Airhart views herself as a community mentor, educator, and lover of all things artistic, with jazz and fine art, including acting, at the top of the list. She's participated in the University of Arkansas-Fort Smith's (UAFS) Shakespeare production of The Twelfth Night, Fort Smith's Little Theaters' The Man Who Came to Dinner, and several short films. Her chap poetry book, Wild and Whirling Words, released in 2014 to great success. Her favorite poem from the book is "Mr. Watermelon Man" because of its connection to her childhood summers in Morrilton, Arkansas. Writing since about age six, her first poem published when she was just twelve-years old in Ebony Jr. Magazine. She didn't share her poetry publicly, however, until 1996 in New York City's famous Nuyorican Poets Cafe. Darneisha wrote a commissioned poem for John Cain (John Cain Foundation) of KABF at 88.3 FM radio station. Most recently, she created the Lyrical Poetry enrichment program.

No Towel to Throw In

BY RICKY ALLEN

Can you imagine never hearing a man say, "You can do it, Son," or "I understand, Son," or "I'm proud of you, Son"?

Can you imagine never having a man present to celebrate your success and comfort you in your failures?

Can you imagine never seeing a man love and take care of his family?

I didn't have to imagine it; I lived it.

Every boy needs a man to guide, correct, and validate him, even if that man is not his dad.

As I reflect on what it means to be a Black man in America, I weep because of life-long oppression and racial injustice. I weep when I see Black-on-Black crime and when people of my race minimize and marginalize one another.

When I watched the 2020 racial injustice ordeals and the Black Lives Matter movement grow, I wrote:

You violated me in the worst way.
My women and children, you took to foreplay.
You took it because you could and thought it was okay.

What is it about yours that makes you want mine?

Aren't you happy with your self-proclaimed shrine?

Open your eyes that you might see the gross injustice you impose upon me.

Open your ears that you might hear how sorrows cry from far and near.

Don't call me brother nor friend

With a smile on your face and a dagger in your hand.

Open your heart that you might feel the awful sting with each unjust ordeal.

These words were a message to fate, my most fierce opponent. The fight for my identity and significance was, at a time, brutal. It was a fight for survival that began when I was four-years- old. This first ordeal nearly took my life.

"Mama, I don't want to die," I said as my mother clenched my small hands.

"Lord, Lord, my baby," Mama said as tears ran down her face.

"Don't cry, Mama. I'll be alright."

"Lord, Lord, my baby," she repeated as she shook her head and rocked back and forth.

I don't know that I understood death at the tender age of four. However, based on what I had seen on TV, people died when someone shot them. The sound from the red sirens on top of the black hearse was earsplitting. Ironically, when I was a little boy, my hometown didn't have colorful ambulances. It used a hearse for both destinations. Where was it taking me? Was I on my way to the hospital or graveyard?

In the sweltering summer of 1967, a single shot rang throughout what was known as "Black Town" in the small, segregated city with a census of approximately 9000 people. My dad had come to Arkansas for a visit. It was the first time he'd seen his four-year-old son. Dad had previously sent my mother and brother from Portland, Oregon, back to Arkansas. He had promised to come back for us. This first visit would be one that consisted of a lifetime of pain.

The grown folks were in the house and had instructed my brother and me to go outside and play. Mama always said, "Kids have no business in grown folks' conversations."

I could only imagine what those conversations were like between a mother and a man who abandoned her pregnant daughter and two-year-old grandson. I could only imagine what the dialogue would have been like for a young mother, who now had the responsibility of raising two boys with no moral or financial support from their daddy.

While they all talked in the tiny two-room shotgun house in an alley off Kentucky Street, my brother and I went outside to play as instructed. *How could he have such a fancy car when we had to walk everywhere unless someone offered us a ride?*

My brother and I got in the car and pretended to take a trip. It was a trip I'd never forget.

I took my place in the driver's seat. My brother, who was now six years old, was in the passenger seat. As we pretended, I noticed my brother exploring the car's console and discovering a gun in it. Immediately, I told him to put the gun down.

I knew it was a gun because my brother and I would watch cowboys and Indians movies on TV and often assumed those roles outside. He was the cowboy. I was the Indian. I told him that I was going to tell my parents that he had a gun.

Suddenly, I heard a loud noise and felt a hot sensation when the bullet entered my four-year-old body right beneath my right armpit and pierced through to exit on the left side, just beneath my heart. I made my way out of the car and to the front door. The next thing I remembered was lying in the backseat of my daddy's car with a green beach towel wrapped around my bleeding body.

My condition was too severe for the local hospital. I needed the care of a trauma center to surgically remove the bullet. Mama and I were in the hearse heading to a trauma center forty-four miles away. A dire situation became worse when the hearse had mechanical problems and broke down midway.

"Mama, I don't want to die," I said.

"Baby, it's going to be okay," she said as tears fell from her face like rain from a dark and fully swollen cloud.

It would be alright because a resident on a hill saw the ambulance in distress and called the Arkansas State Police. I remembered the state trooper showing up in a hat like Yogi the Bear and saving the day. He placed me in the back seat of his car and completed the journey to the trauma center.

Was this the first indication that I wasn't on my way to the graveyard? Had my Creator destined me for greatness, and no bullet nor broken down hearse would stop me from arriving?

Doctors at the trauma center successfully removed the bullet. They were amazed that the bullet entered and traveled through my body without damaging any vital organs. Mama called the intervention divine.

The day I got shot changed my relationship with my brother. I knew it was an accident, but the outcome for me was more detrimental than the event. My brother endured the cruelty of some who suggested that I might die, which would have been his fault. He went into a state of situational depression. I recovered fully from the gunshot, but my brother did not. Instead of being his little brother, someone to laugh and play with, I became an object for him to protect. He treated me as if I were fragile and chose other playmates.

I wanted his friendship more than his protection. I felt the two male figures I needed the most at this young age had left me. I thought that they didn't like me, and I became increasingly vulnerable and just wanted to be accepted.

I would wait until Mama would go to sleep after a long, tiring night of work and sneak off to other boys' houses to play. Mama would wake up looking for me. When she found me or I returned home, it wasn't good.

"But you said I could go," I said, thinking it was okay because I had asked, and she said yes.

"How many times have I told you not to ask me to go anywhere when I'm trying to sleep," she'd respond.

This behavior plagued me most of my boyhood and contributed to most of my childhood whippings. When I wasn't sneaking off, I hung around the house and learned to play by myself. When I didn't want to play alone, I turned to my sister, who was fourteen months younger than me. She didn't want to play with cars, trucks, and bugs; she preferred dolls. So, together we played with dolls. I remember us playing with the Baby Alive doll, that was life-like in that it cooed, giggled, ate, peed, and even pooped. Not only did playing with this doll provide a little girl practice in being a good big sister and someday mommy, but it also offered a little red-headed boy practice in being a good big brother and ultimately a good father. Yes, I played with dolls. I learned to give them bottles, comb their hair, change their diapers, clothe them, and quiet them when they cried.

I also remember the many days spent sitting at her play table with the miniature tea set, sipping a little bit of tea, and having a family dinner. My sister and I sat at the table, ate and talked about our day. The power of imagination lends to the possibility of realization.

This playtime created a vision of having a family someday. At a young age, I decided that I was going to be a loving husband and father. I decided that I would treat the women in my life with dignity and respect. I decided I would give my family the best my money could buy.

I grew up hearing boys don't cry, and they certainly don't play with dolls. More important than playing with dolls was building a loving, trusting, and enduring relationship with my sister. Through this playtime, I learned the lessons of sacrificial love, healthy boundaries, and uncompromising respect. Was playing with dolls such a bad thing?

Growing up was hard for me. It was like being in a foreign country without a tour guide. I didn't know where to start or what to do. My boyhood and childhood created an incredible pursuit for manhood.

I realize now it is my responsibility to share what I've learned to equip and encourage boys to grow into responsible men and empower some men to remove boyhood chains.

I recall a man once asking me a question in response to my struggles, "Have you thrown in the towel?"

I stood there with tears in my eyes and responded, "I don't have a towel to throw in."

It would have been easier to mask my pain and hide behind anger and disappointment. Or use the fact that I grew up without a daddy or experienced some negative things as reasons for me to give up.

But I know I am not alone in my experiences. I don't carry a white towel to wave in surrender. The proverbial towel I carry is green and stained by blood, tears, and sweat. Its green color represents life. The stains are a reminder of all that I've gone through to live. It is a towel cleansed by renewed purpose. I use this towel to wipe up the mess of childhood abandonment, neglect, and abuse.

I use this towel to wipe my brow and press on to be the man my Creator has intended.

I now lend this towel to the male who's had a journey like mine.

Author Ricky Allen, owner and CEO of RELATE LLC, has a delightful and unique way of helping readers translate common-sense concepts into common practices. The residual effect for his audience is not merely entertainment but also enlightening. He has twelve published books. Learn more about this visionary author by visiting his website www.relatellc.com.

His Garden at Night

BY MARLA CANTRELL

Our land wasn't the prettiest place you'd ever seen—nine acres between a busy two-lane highway and an interstate. The ground was red clay that stayed wet except for July and August when it cracked mightily from the extreme heat. There was an abandoned pear grove, gone to ruin, behind a scruff of briars and a field of Johnson grass as sharp as razors when you ran through it.

At the front of the property were my grandmother's two modest houses—one she lived in and one she rented to her nephew, Bud, who'd suffered a brain injury in a drunk driving accident. Bud, a man in his mid-forties, had been the one drinking. On our land, he became infatuated with old TV picture tubes, buying as many as he could at a nearby auction, then spending hours using them for target practice. Late afternoons were punctuated by the boom, boom, boom of Bud's old .22 and his laughter that always followed.

No one ever thought to rein him in.

My family of five lived 200 yards behind Grandma and Bud in a trailer we'd bought from a woman who must have loved the ocean. All the blue curtains, in place throughout the house, had brightly painted plastic pins of tall ships attached, each at least four inches wide. Those pins, set at odd angles, rode our curtains as if crossing rough seas. I imagined the pins on the bosom of an old woman's dress, where the waters were wide and steady.

No one ever thought to change them.

One summer, my mother bought an old wood-burning cooking stove and set it up outside. She seemed happier that Arkansas summer, freed from cooking in a trailer without air-conditioning. I'd sit on our rickety wooden front steps and eat pork chops or fried potatoes and an ear or two of sweet corn that my dad grew in his massive garden.

In the daylight hours of every summer, my brother, sister, mom, and I picked tomatoes for a commercial farmer. Our forearms carried the green itchy stain of the vines and the sharp, chemical smell of those summer plants. At eleven years of age, I worked hard.

No one ever asked me to tend the garden at home.

One night, I saw the garden transform. Or, more accurately, I saw my father change. He was a man with the body of a welterweight boxer, sometimes gentle, often moody, with a temper bigger than he was. Before I'd lost my baby teeth, I became alert to the weather warnings of his changing disposition.

No one ever blamed him; he'd seen combat in Okinawa. He'd barely survived a world war.

If I'd known the word enigma, I would have used it then. My gentle dad. My angry dad. The same man. At eleven, my vocabulary failed me. I only knew how my throat tightened when I noticed my father's jaw set in a certain way. How I read him like a barometer, always ready for the storm.

The night I'm remembering was a scorcher. I'd moved into the hallway, blanket and pillow in tow, hoping to catch a breeze from the water-cooled fan that sat in our living room window and blew in that direction. My sister, on the top bunk of our room, didn't stir when I left. Our bedrooms had flimsy pocket doors, and from behind my brother's, I could hear the St. Louis Cardinals game playing on his transistor radio. My brother was a Roger Maris fan, and I listened for his name to be called.

Eventually, the house grew still, the baseball game over. I roamed, feeling the power of being alone. I got a drink from the tap. I opened the refrigerator door. In the freezer, I found ice milk—we were too poor for ice cream—and scooped out a bowlful.

Tree frogs are loud when the rest of the world is quiet. They sang, and I listened. Wanting to hear more, I dropped my bowl in the sink, eased open the front door, and sat down.

I have always lived half in this world and half in a world of my making. That night, sitting on the wooden steps, I was a saloon girl, pink plumes in my hair, about to be rushed from danger by a good-at-heart gunslinger. The story was playing out in the most perfect way when I saw headlights approaching.

I made myself small, hoping the lights wouldn't find me. When the headlights got closer, I saw it was my father's 1960 Chevy pickup, turquoise in color, still pretty after eight years in his care.

If I had looked at a clock, I would have realized it was time for Dad to come home. He worked the night shift at a furniture factory in the next town over and had for years. But I was not a practical child, often startled by routine events.

The path to our trailer was rutted, and the truck bounced along. When he got several yards away, he veered into the pasture. When he neared his garden, he circled around, stopping where I had the perfect view of him. He kept the lights on.

My father was not a large man, but he had big, square hands, strong arms, a solid chest. In the back of the truck were two fifty-five-gallon barrels. I knew he kept the barrels beside my grandmother's house, catching rainwater, but I had never seen what he did with them next.

My father did not hurry. He'd learned to move at one speed from a man he worked with in a Texas quarry, back when he was just a kid hitchhiking, picking up odd jobs along the way. On his first day, my father had lifted rock after rock, straining against them, working until he nearly passed out. An old-timer found my father doubled over, searching for breath.

"New guys like you always got something to prove," he said to my father. "They'll send you home now, and you won't make a full day's pay." The man rubbed the thumb and forefinger of his right hand together. "Me, though, I'll be here at quitting time to collect the dough."

When my dad asked him what he'd done wrong, the man told him it was all in the pacing. "Find a rhythm and stick to it, and don't give a dadburn what nobody else thinks."

No one ever had to tell my father again.

So, my dad moseyed around the truck. He let down the tailgate and sat. From where I was, I could see him take a cigarette from his shirt pocket. I saw him strike a match and watched him ignite the amber ember of his smoke.

Away from the concerns of his family, his shoulders loosened and fell. He swung his feet the way I did, sitting on a fishing dock. After a few minutes, the cigarette went dark, and my dad got down from the tailgate.

I watched him belly-up to the first barrel. He gripped it, leaned back for leverage, and moved the sloshing barrel side to side until he had it in his arms. With a grunt, he lowered it to the ground. He kept a tin pail, the size of a mop bucket, with a rope attached to the handle, in the bed of his truck. He got it out, dipped it into the rainwater, and got to work.

My parents listened to Loretta Lynn, Jim Reeves, and Ernest Tubb, so I was surprised when my dad began singing "Oh, What A Beautiful Morning" from the musical *Oklahoma*. He sang. He dipped. He watered. When he got to the line about the corn being as tall as an elephant, he was at the end of the first row, illuminated by both the truck lights and the moon. He swung the now-empty pail above his head in a circle and laughed, the sound like a bell choir. When the first barrel was nearly empty, he tipped it over, then manhandled the second and started again.

Ours was not always an easy life, and we needed the food he grew. That's what I'd thought the garden meant. Yet on that night, there was nothing utilitarian in what I saw. The water bucket was a harp in his hand. The rain barrels were trumpets. I watched the rhythm of his gait, the way he stopped to ruffle a corn plant—the way he took three ears of corn and tossed them in the air like a juggler.

No one ever told me my dad could be like this.

When he finished, he loaded the barrels in the truck bed. He sat again on the tailgate and lit another cigarette. Above him, the world was navy blue; the stars were shards of light that blinked and swam.

My father craned his neck to look up. On the porch, I did the same. The Cardinals had won that night. In a few months, they'd lose the World Series to the Detroit Tigers, but that night they were still riding high.

Some things, I realized, moved beyond us, landed in the sky, blessed us from above. The sound of a baseball connecting with a wooden bat was one; the hush of treefrogs when my father sang, another.

When my father jumped from the tailgate, I slid inside the house, suddenly afraid to be caught watching him. I'd been bitten by mosquitos, and my legs and arms were dotted with welts. I grabbed my blanket and pillow from the hallway and slipped into my room.

Not long after, the front door opened. My father sighed, and the heaviness he often brought into our house returned. The kitchen light went on. I heard the coffee pot a little later, the percolator sounding like maracas from where I lay. I never understood him drinking coffee so late at night, but there were many things I didn't understand about my father.

The next morning, we walked the two miles to the tomato field while my father slept. We passed Bud, who was carrying another TV picture tube, setting it beside three more he'd placed in a row. The gunfire would come later, tiny explosions that punctuated most days.

My grandmother came out of her house, coffee cup in hand. Her robe was purple chenille with an image of a peacock covering the back. She raised her hand to us, a queen to her subjects, and I noticed for the first time how small she was.

In the field that day, I battled tomato vines. I carried buckets down long rows, filling them again and again with fat tomatoes. This garden was a beast, a master, a torment.

When we got home, my father had already gone to work.

Outside, his garden swayed in the hot breeze. The garden was mostly corn. A few tomatoes. Bell peppers. Hot peppers. The rows were neat and tended. Not a weed in sight. Not a broken plant. Nothing overripe.

I looked down at my hands. I had dirt under my fingernails. I traced the ragged scar on my left knee, a reminder of the damage a barbed-wire fence could do. What a mess I was, the daughter who often nagged her father for tiny shows of affection, for his attention, for a sign he loved her.

No one had to tell me I wasn't perfect.

That garden, though, was. And my father was its holy shepherd. I had seen his worship service, the one-man choir, the attitude of prayer in a man who stayed home to sleep while the rest of us attended church every Sunday.

No one had to tell me to remember it.

I've kept that night in my pocket all these years. I have since worshipped under a canopy of pines, at the edges of oceans, on my family's land, where the grass always smelled of sour apple chewing gum and wild garlic. I tell myself I knew my father in a way no one else did because of a garden, ripe for the picking, being tended in the dead of night.

Marla Cantrell is a writer, editor, and creative writing instructor. Her short story collection, Early Morning in the Land of Dreams, was published in 2020, and in 2021, her book won the Arkansas Library Association's Arkansiana Award for Adult Fiction. She also received an Arkansas Arts Council Fellowship Award in Short Fiction. Marla lives with her husband and their enthusiastic miniature schnauzer, Happy Wigglesworth, in a spot with the perfect view of the Boston Mountains.

The Do-Right Bug

BY JILL COX-CORDOVA

From March 10 until June 12, 2020, I embraced staying inside my home located in Kennesaw, Georgia, just 28 miles north of Atlanta. My neighborhood has a roundabout that might as well be railroad tracks. On one side, progressive college students rent, and people of color— either retired or who currently teach like me—reside in three-to-four bedroom homes built in the 80s. The tree-lined lots are about an acre surrounded by pine, oak, and sweet gumball-bearing trees. On the other end of the roundabout, the yards have been filled with Trump signs since 2016. But that was not what kept me, a Black woman, inside. Fear had invaded my body, and each day, it snuffed out my willingness to face COVID-19.

Convinced that it—a monster worse than any child could imagine—waited for me outside my door, I prayed that my mother, who still enjoyed grocery shopping, would return unharmed to the home my husband and I shared with her.

My workload lightened because my three in-person Composition II courses at Georgia's third-largest university became online, asynchronous ones. Stillness arrived, too, until I realized that it came with a surround sound of my own voice trying to silence deafening thoughts that things will worsen.

It did.

Every newscast I watched showcased COVID-related deaths…and the murders of Black people.

Take Breonna Taylor, for example, who was shot to death in her own apartment in Louisville, Kentucky. That is where I earned my MFA in 2017 and gained countless memories in my developmental years going to holiday parades and people watching at White Castle with my mother and grandmother. My grandmother's house in Hodgenville was just an hour south of Louisville, and I grew up an hour south of her in Mammoth Cave National Park.

My family knew a lot of Taylors, too, so I took a closer look at Breonna's bright brown eyes and easy smile. I did not know her specifically, but I recognized her as a Black woman like me, just trying to survive and do all the right things to thrive. That made her—us—targets.

My own tear-filled eyes darted around the room as if the walls held the answers of how to stop those who try to erase us. *That could be any of us, no matter where we live.*

I had to do something, but what? My health conditions prevented me from joining street protestors. I no longer worked at CNN or any other TV networks, so telling stories at that level was out, too. I tried to determine other ways to be an activist, but no ideas came to the rescue. It was as if my core existence were chained; my tongue shackled. Silenced. I thought sleeping on it would help, but few who are woke can do that. Plus, Breonna Taylor had been in her bed when police barged into her apartment.

I must have managed a few hours of sleep because I had a dream about a woman I had never seen before. She had gray hair cut in a chic bob that touched her shoulders. Her dark brown face was long, lean, and chiseled. She wore prescription glasses that looked like they changed into shades if she were in the sun. Her short-sleeved, white blouse revealed toned, but not too muscular arms.

The next day I wrote about that description and called her Faye/Flo. I still had no real sense of who she was nor her situation, but I believed I was supposed to write about her.

"Have you tried googling Faye and Flo?" my husband asked.

I took the hint and entered *Faye AND Flo* into the search bar.

I gasped when I saw the results: *The Other Kennedys* popped up first. Faye and Flo were two Black women and sisters originally from Missouri. They had three other sisters, but Faye and Flo had both spent their adulthoods fighting oppressors. Flo, a Black feminist, and a founder of the National Organization of Women (NOW) had often spoken on the same stages as Gloria Steinem.

Faye had famous friends, too. Former President Barack Obama wrote a letter expressing his condolences after she died on February 28, 2020. His letter said in part, "Faye knew what it was to dig just a little deeper, to extend her hand just a little further . . . because she believed that over time, if we all did that, if we all tried to alleviate another person's suffering, just a little bit… then we would all prevail."

More and more research about Faye and Flo supported that belief, this notion that warriors against injustices are stronger when they work together. Yet, I was still sitting in my house wondering what *I* could contribute to become an everyday activist.

That changed on May 25, 2020, when I watched the video of George Floyd's murder. That was the same day that the so-called "Central Park Karen" called police to say a Black man was threatening her when, in reality, he had politely asked her to put a leash on her dog.

Enough, I thought. COVID-19 didn't catch me; the do-right bug did.

On June 12, 2020, I put on a mask, got in my car, and went to downtown Kennesaw to Wildman's, known for selling Confederate flags. My goal was to talk to the owner. After all, sometimes dialogues lead to positive action.

A small sign on the front door said, "Leave Your Hate Outside," which made me wonder what their word was for the content of the store's interior.

My nose was the first to detect a layer of dust as thick as a sheet of construction paper on the least expensive items, $1 Confederate flag pens and buttons. I sneezed. If only people were allergic to hatred.

The owner, 89, looked frail with his gray-white beard long enough to reach his thin chest. He dragged his right leg like it hurt to move it any other way. Still, I was sure he could win a game of quick draw with the two guns on each side of his waist.

I noticed the "Wanted: Negroes" tee-shirts hanging just under a bulletin board plastered with polaroid shots of smiling Black people. Props.

At the back of the store, I spotted a mannequin clad in Ku Klux Klan attire. Its hood was dingy, decades old. In the eye cutouts, the eyes of an ape mask gazed at me. To my 4'11 frame, it seemed over 6-foot tall. Pinned to one side of the robe was a white tag with black, handwritten letters that said "1920's New England Order of Protection." A blood-red sash dangled from its right shoulder, while a noose hung like graduation honor cords.

I wanted to scream, cry, *speak.* I couldn't. It was my first time seeing a display of hatred like that, but not the first time I had come face to face with a Klansman.

That happened during my 20's when I worked as a newscast producer in Charlotte, North Carolina. I had called and booked the head of the local Klan and the NAACP to have an on-air debate about David Duke's run for political office. When they had arrived, both were dressed in three-piece suits; the Klansman's was beige, the NAACP guy's was blue. I extended my hand to greet each one. The Klansman had grunted and refused to shake my hand. Later, his assistant invited me to his birthday party… in a barn in an area so remote, it had no street name.

I didn't go.

While at Wildman's, that morning's tea bubbled inside my stomach and rushed to my throat. Struggling to form sentences, I managed to ask the store employee, "Why display this?"

"Cause the mannequin would be naked," she answered.

When I did not laugh with her, she said she once thought that the hood was a dunce cap.

I stared at her.

Later, she returned that look when she said people should be thankful that it is 2020 and not 1820. "Aren't you glad slavery is over?" she asked.

"Is it?" I asked.

History cannot be changed, we agreed. In 1993, the Kennesaw Historical Society even awarded Wildman's owner with its Historical Preservation Award. But what people in this store called a "dose of history" cease being historical memorabilia when it is embedded into a belief system and actively practiced. *That* is hatred, and, in this case, it had an actual price tag.

I heard shuffling and spotted the owner coming toward me. The pace of my heartbeat now matched that of an Olympic sprinter, so I breathed like a yogi to try to calm myself.

In a matter-of-fact tone, he said, "I know people have called me racist." His voice was soft, much to my surprise. I had expected him to roar like a monster.

"How does that make you feel?" I asked.

He shrugged. "I welcome everyone. Green, yellow, striped, Martian. I don't care. I have no qualms against race, religion. sexual preference. Business is booming."

Goosebumps appeared on my arm, and I rubbed them. I forced myself to look at his weathered face, which did not alarm me as much as his blue eyes, foggy with intolerance. The message was still clear, though: he would shoot me if I said, looked, or did the wrong thing. I put my feet together like I was getting in formation and asked, "Would you consider removing anything others deem offensive?"

He shook his head. "I wouldn't go to your house and ask you if you're getting rid of that thing I don't like."

He looked me up and down before he shuffled to another part of the store. "I want to show you something," he called over his shoulder.

My heart did a high jump. I wondered if he were going to return with another, bigger weapon. My instincts told me to scan the room for something I could use to protect myself, but I more frightened of taking my eyes off him.

I saw him pick up a 5x7 framed photo.

He was laughing with his whole body when he shoved it at me. The photo was black and white. A young boy, maybe six, with blonde curly hair was wearing shorts and a short-sleeved, button-down shirt.

"Know who that is?"

I shook my head.

"That's me," he guffawed.

"What is so funny?"

"My mother made that outfit from my father's Klan robe when we could no longer afford the dues."

We stared at each other.

If he had not told me that story, I would have just viewed the picture like that of any other kid. I knew he was trying to scare me. The killing season of Blacks is year-round, after all. His proud racist beliefs appeared to be cemented into his old brain, his being. I did not think I could change that. I decided it would be easier—as difficult as it is—to try to dismantle systems designed to keep the oppressed down, in a permanent position.

I felt Faye's presence circle around me like a force field. Then the chains around my existence and shackles on my tongue popped and released me. Oh, how I wanted to dance and jump and shout. Courage had clicked inside me like a switch now stuck on doing more, saying more about all the injustices I witnessed, experienced, or heard.

I realized I already had the ability to use my gifts and talents to help the oppressed, those in need. Now I had the will. That was activism to me. I smiled and silently thanked Faye for motivating me to go in there.

"What are you grinning at?" Myers asked with a hint of alarm.

"I know who you are," I said. "But you have no idea who I am."

I sashayed out like a supermodel to Prince's "Emancipation" playing on a loop in my head.

Yes, I was now free, my voice unleashed by the do-right bug.

Jill Cox-Cordova holds an MFA from Spalding University in Louisville, Kentucky; a master's degree in broadcast journalism from Northwestern University; and a bachelor's degree from Macalester College in St. Paul, Minnesota. She worked as a journalist for twenty-one years at such media outlets as CNN.com, The Weather Channel, and MSNBC. She also freelanced for Essence magazine. Her creative writing publication credentials include flash fiction in an anthology and creative nonfiction in Parks and Points. She works as a professional development instructor but also conducts in-person and online workshops, plus editing services for first-time and established authors. She co-hosts with her husband, "I'm Right. I'm Right," a podcast about relationships.

My Neighborhood, My World

BY TANJA ENOCH

London, Paris, Rome and the Caribbean are just a few travel destinations that make for adventure and the expanding of one's view of the world. Some get to travel to these and other places, but many don't. Some would say they, therefore, have a limited view of the world. Not getting to travel and see the world, especially in your formative years, can be viewed as unfortunate. However, I don't think that's necessarily so. Traveling and learning of other spaces, places and cultures, yes, is good. But having your neighborhood be your world during your formative years can be a positive thing.

Neighborhoods can be shelters that guard their young, much like the eagle, until they are ready to fly. That's how I viewed my neighborhood—the one of my formative years. It had all the necessities of life—family, friends, food, shelter, school, and adventure—within a three-block radius in all directions.

The South End was my world. The two things that were instrumental in shaping my worldview were within feet of each other. My family was one. Within a few feet from our home and over one cross street stood the other, my elementary school. During second grade, I could look out my classroom window and see my house. And so could my teacher. Can't be late, can't be mischievous, can't say my mom's not home. Just look out the window and do a fact check.

There is also security in looking out that same classroom window and seeing my mom or dad, sister, or brother arriving home or walking over to pick me up.

Look in the opposite direction from my home's front window, and up the street is where I spent many a Saturday. When it was time for me to get my hair straightened on an early Saturday morning, my mom got me up, ready, and out the front door, watching as I walked the half block up to Ms. Maudie's beauty shop. I would cross to the other side of the street, go up two houses, walk down her driveway past her car and her house, before arriving at the small building in the back.

It was a nice setup, a mini house. It had a small waiting area with a couch and TV. From the couch, you could look into a large room that had one chair pushed up to a bowl for washing hair. Next to it was another chair with a hairdryer attached to the back of it. That's the chair where I would take naps while my hair was drying. Many a time, Ms. Maudie would have to nudge me and say, "Hold your head up so your front can dry." That was usually my second nap because I would take my first one on the couch as I awaited my turn.

After I had read the book that I had brought with me, watched a little TV, and ran a quick errand into Ms. Maudie's house to get something she had forgotten, I would curl up on the couch and wait for her to do the hair of all the older ladies that had appointments after mine. They knew that I lived right down the street, and I knew that although I had gotten there first, they would be taken care of ahead of me. These blue-haired ladies always had a story to tell and an opinion to give. But I stayed in my place, kept quiet, often listening to the stories as I fell asleep. Finally, my turn came. It was often evening time when my hair was done. Time to close up the shop. I would walk with Ms. Maudie to her back door, and she would watch me until I got safely to my front door.

If I didn't spend Saturdays with Ms. Maudie, I would get sent to the neighborhood store for something. Of course, that something would vary, and who I was getting the something for also changed. I was the youngest, so my mother, father, brother or sister would tell me to go to the store for them. I didn't mind, though, because it gave me a chance to go on an adventure. Do I take the street way to the store, or do I cut across the school ground and make a stop at my friend's house that was on the other side, past the school fence? It was also nice that my friend lived next door to the store.

I would eventually get to the purpose of my trip. I wasn't concerned about whether the store was open or closed since the owner lived across the street from it. She knew me and everyone else in the neighborhood. If the store weren't open, I would go right across the street, walk up her driveway, pass her car and knock on her back door. If she were busy, I would hear through the door, "Ok, I will be over in a minute."

Crossing back over to the store, I would just wait outside or visit with my friend until she came to open it. I would get what I needed, pay or ask her to put it on our tab, and then cut across the schoolground on my way back home.

That area was the biggest part of my adventures. It provided hours of exploration above and below ground. Below ground was a drainage tunnel that ran across the length of the school property. The opening to the tunnel was at the front of the school. When it wasn't raining, it was the place to search for buried treasures. Sometimes others would be there playing, and one would say, "Race you to the other end."

The ones above would take off running. Those of us in the tunnel would run at high speed to the other end. I don't remember me or any of the others having a flashlight nor it being totally dark in the tunnel. I do, however, recall it being loads of fun and adventure.

Above ground was my favorite spot for fun: the slide. It wasn't a regular slide. Instead, it was my hideaway, my spot for daydreaming. The top of the slide had a covered landing where I could sit, stare up into the clouds, and wonder about things beyond my neighborhood and the possibility of another child far away looking up at that same sky and daydreaming.

There was not a longing to leave my neighborhood when I was in my favorite spot. There was just a knowing that there were other places outside of my safe space. I knew that one day I would venture out to explore some of those places. But back then, I was at home in my world. It nurtured me. It sheltered me. It fortified me for the world outside my neighborhood. Thanks, South End.

Tanja Enoch is a student of the art of storytelling. Be it written, a photograph or a video, for her it's about sharing memories. From winning an essay contest in elementary school, to being on the yearbook staff in high school and having a career in cable and television broadcasting, she likes to capture a story. She is a Ph.D. student in the Heritage Studies Program at Arkansas State University in Jonesboro, Arkansas. Her goal is to combine her background in media with her doctoral studies to produce documentaries that tell the stories of African Americans in the lower Arkansas Delta region.

Mama's Tale

BY ANGELA GRIFFITH-NEWKIRK

She stood five feet, four inches tall and weighed about ninety pounds. Her body had taken a beating from surgeries and medication prescribed to keep her alive. Her beautiful brown skin covered the shell that housed a heart that was full of life, compassion, and love. She got mad if you did not put "Mrs." in front of her name, Mrs. Mary Elizabeth Williams Griffith.

Her diagnosis was not promising. I wanted her to spend whatever time God had allotted her with me. She was supposed to spend time with me. I had moved to Houston, Texas. On this day, I was going to get and bring her home with me. I was looking forward to pajama parties, slap-your-leg laughter, cooking tasty food, and shopping at her favorite store, Dollar Tree. I anticipated us shooting the breeze—just spending quality time together. Unbeknownst to me, Mama was preparing herself for a different trip, not the one I had in my mind.

Whenever I listened to Daddy talk about her, it warmed my heart. He and I sat in the dining room one day looking at old yearbooks. "Your mama was real smart," he said. "She was almost a genius."

He smiled as we thumbed through the pages of a well-kept yearbook from the Arkansas Agricultural, Mechanical and Normal University (AM&N and currently the University of Arkansas at Pine Bluff). They attended college there. Daddy played baseball, and Mama pledged Zeta Phi Beta sorority. I liked the enthusiasm in his voice when he spoke of her—after sixty-two years of marriage, he was still in love, and it showed. "She graduated high school when she was 15 years old."

Mama had beauty to match her intellect; I wondered which of the two was responsible for his unwavering love for her. Mama was crowned Ouachita County High School Homecoming Queen. Her portrait was once on display at the Mosaic Templars Cultural Museum in Little Rock, Arkansas. More importantly, she will forever be displayed in Daddy's heart.

Mama was a woman of versatility. In the morning, she would be outside the barn cleaning chitterlings. Hours later, with a mirror and a screwdriver, she would fix a floor model television. The next day, she would tend to the vegetables in her garden, water her many plants, and serve delicious homemade ice cream. She decorated cakes for weddings and special occasions and took photos and videos, too.

I looked at her hands and smiled as I thought about my tenth birthday party at Grandma Classie's house. I traced her fingers gently. These were the same hands that created a beautiful castle cake for me. I wiped tears away when I thought of the details of the cake, how she masterfully created it—just to make me happy. I was happy. She had a knack for making people feel special. Hospitality was one of her many gifts. She juggled her responsibilities as a mother, wife, Sunday School

Superintendent, Youth Director, 4-H Club advisor, Master Gardner, Librarian, and so much more.

Mama was the second oldest of eleven children. When her mother passed away from cancer, she became a mother figure to her siblings. Her house became the gathering place, where the French toast was delicious, the coffee was hot, the warm banana pudding was satisfying, and the laughter was welcoming.

Mama brilliantly instilled the lessons she learned in all her children. I remember when I was preparing to speak at a 4-H public speaking competition, Mama said, "Take your speech to the podium."

I had practiced in front of my horses and had memorized my speech, so I respectfully said, "I don't need to."

Just as sure as coal is black, I stood behind the lectern with no words. Every word I had committed to memory disappeared. Gone. I was devastated. That was the day Mama taught me a lesson in obedience, humility, and responsibility all in one. She had every right to chastise me. She could have cut me with words as sharp as a butcher's knife. She did not. She didn't say I told you so. This was a testament to her caring loving nature.

Thoughts of Mama kept me company as I drove. I preferred the thoughts of a vibrant Mama—filled with creativity who planned and organized. The mama who told stories and dressed up like a witch at Halloween, and a bunny at Easter, and who used to offer a kiss to men in the form of a Hershey's Kiss. "Sir, would you like a kiss?" she would ask. When they perked up to pucker up, she quickly laid a Hershey's Kiss in their hand. Although she did it multiple times, we still found it amusing.

The navigation system took me on a route that was foreign and scary, but I was determined to get there. I refused to make multiple stops because I had a mission in mind. I was going to get Mama.

I finally arrived, and I was famished. I was not as prepared as I should have been, so my girlfriend Carolyn met me at the Walgreens near my sister's house, so that she could hand off a blanket and a salad for me.

When I made it to my sister's house where my mom was staying, I was surprised to find Mama in a hospital bed. The dementia had taken a toll on her. There were days she knew me and days that she did not. I was hoping this was the day she did.

"Hey Mama," I said.

She responded with a dry greeting. I assumed it was fatigue that had set in because it was around 9:30 p.m. I went round and round with her, trying to convince her that I was her baby girl and I had come to take her back home with me. She was unbothered by my musings.

I showed her pictures of my Christmas tree, and she responded in a way that was crass.

"That don't look like nothing," she said. Whatever came up in Mama's mind came out.

Trying not to let her comment get under my skin, I told myself that it was all my fault for purchasing a white tree with a small budget for decorations. I was not as gifted at decorating trees like my friend, Dovie, who had twenty-five trees in her home, and Mama was fascinated with each one of them. I just wanted her to like my one tree. Although I was no longer a little girl, I still needed, wanted, and desired my mama's approval.

I sat there in a tizzy trying to figure out what I could have done to make the tree look better. I kept staring at the picture on my phone, the tree that did not look like anything, according to Mama. I decided to show Mama my cousin Sharon's Christmas tree.

"That don't look like nothing either!" she snapped. I was relieved that she didn't approve of her tree either.

I was happy to be in Mama's presence. I could hardly sleep. I was elated to occupy the same space with the lady who gave birth to me. She was wise, intuitive, and delightful.

She created a purposeful life and not just a living for herself. She was always ensuring that everyone around her was okay.

She was the first entrepreneur to influence me. I felt enriched because of the contributions she made to her family, church, and community. She owned Pine Manor Printing. She was the one who planned family reunions and milestone events. She had designed and printed church and funeral programs for her surrounding community. She never raised her prices. Until her failing health, people could get a hundred programs for the mere price of twenty-five dollars. I got my creativity from her.

By her bedside, I sat and reflected on her life. It was evident that her last days were near. I pulled the recliner closer to her bed and wrapped my arm around her. It was uncomfortable to stay in that position, but I didn't mind, I just wanted to be close to her.

I called my friend who had just lost both her parents. She said, "I know you want everything to be perfect when your mom transitions, but this ain't even about you. This is between your mama and God. You need to stay out of their business."

This revelation gave me peace. This was Mama and God's business.

I was so happy that she got a chance to spend quality time with her children and grandchildren those last days. She hadn't eaten in weeks, and when she saw my dad for the last time, she asked, "What have you been eating?"

She was showing compassion to the man she loved. The same woman who had skipped multiple meals in the last four weeks wanted to make sure that the love of her life was fed. This was Mama, sharing a final lesson. Wow! She had been a caregiver to many of her family members, and now the time had come for care to be given to her.

My sister Gayle and her children were blessed to share precious moments with her and to connect on a deeper level. Her great-granddaughter, Zuri, had become her pride and joy as they spent hours getting acquainted. She was a bright light in a dark world, but dementia/Alzheimer's sought to snuff Mama's light out completely. Mundane tasks became frustrating, and she became combative and defiant. She was once the life of the party and because of her deterioration, she lacked the vibrance that once penetrated the atmosphere.

I thought about the green Bible Mama carried. It had a caterpillar on it and an inscription that read, "Please be patient with me; God is not finished with me yet."

Patience was one of her virtues. She created and crafted a life that was like a beautiful mosaic. Her friends and family had a front-row seat to her grandeur. We were all glad to be there. Her quick wit was inviting most of the time. Mama had many sayings and clever comebacks that would leave everybody in stitches. She was not going to be outdone or outwitted.

Mama was real, regal, righteous, and remarkable. She was a history maker, mover, and shaker. She served in the church with a genuinely warm spirit. She submitted to God's will and looked fabulous while doing so. She embodied resilience, endured four brain tumor surgeries, and beat colon cancer twice. She was the poster child for perseverance.

My mother navigated the tough terrains of society and moved gracefully from failure to success, with the latter being her lot. The walls of her home were adorned with plaques, certificates, and commendations. She was an overcomer. I will always applaud Mama's pursuit of excellence.

Her sound wisdom continues to resonate with me. I am in awe of her talents and gifts. Her confidence, love, and steadfastness are unmatched. Her ease of bouncing back after every setback and gliding over all personal and public challenges is noteworthy.

As she lay still in her bed, she would occasionally lift her hands toward the ceiling. Maybe she was welcoming the angels to take her to heaven.

"Mama, I love you," I exclaimed.

There was silence. Her once imaginative and powerful mind was baffling as she carefully strategized, implemented, and charted a course to a different place than my house. I just wish that her unfolding story could have ended another way.

She was supposed to come and spend some time with me. I was looking forward to pajama parties, slap-your-leg laughter, cooking tasty food, and shopping at her favorite store, Dollar Tree. I anticipated us shooting the breeze and just spending quality time together.

Without anyone's permission or approval, Mama took a detour. She closed her eyes for the last time on a cool December morning just before the dew set in.

She is now resting in eternity.

Angela Griffith-Newkirk is a proud native of Eagle Mills, Arkansas. She holds a Master of Arts degree in Liberal Studies from Grambling State University and a Bachelor of Arts degree in Speech and Dramatic Arts from the University of Arkansas at Pine Bluff. She is a seasoned educator and was inducted into the Southeast Arkansas Historical Society Black History Hall of Fame for her contribution to the arts. Additionally, she received the Timeless Dreamer and Life Toucher Award in her home state of Arkansas. She is a playwright, workshop presenter, youth advocate and speaker. Her quest for excellence is a continuous journey as she is pursuing a Non-Profit Executive in Leadership Certification from Rice University. She recently received a Certification in Diversity, Equity, and Inclusion from the University of South Florida. She currently serves as the Executive Director for the She Is A CEO Foundation in Houston, Texas. She resides in Katy, Texas, with her husband and 15-year-old son.

To Save My Soul

BY BRYON HODGES

I was in bed just going to sleep when I noticed fog coming into my room under the door. I continued to lay in bed, growing nervous, and then the door opened. Not one, but seven angels entered my room.

The first spoke and said, "Come, for you have been asked for." That was Gabriel.

God is my strength.

I said, "You have the wrong person. Can't be me."

But Gabriel spoke once more, "Come."

So, I got up and walked toward the door, but, to my surprise, there was a white horse and shield with a golden sword. They were given to me (by God). Also, I could see my wife ironing my knight's uniform.

"Why should I need this?" I asked.

"Many will not want you to succeed on your journey," Gabriel explained. "They will do battle with us and stop you from reaching your goal of seeking the Lord, thy God. This is the promise that you find Him and rest your weary soul.

He is one source of rest because your yoke and burden will be light to one who diligently seeks."

So, I put on my knight's uniform that my wife gave me and mounted the great white horse. We rode right through the kitchen wall and did battle with the tempters and many whose wish was to keep me from my true cause, which was to seek and find (to him who knocks the door will be opened.)

After the battles of many, we reached a great white ship on the sea near the beach. We dismounted our horses and Gabriel said, "He is waiting for you."

So, I walked up the plank and He (Jesus) was there. I got down on my knees and was trembling.

He said, "Rise and speak."

"Why am I here?" I asked.

He said, "Your faith has brought you here to find and seek your heart's desires, and it shall be given. Take this net and cast it in the sea for we will seek and find."

I cast the net and pulled it back to me. It was so heavy, but as I pulled it to me, it got lighter and lighter. I asked the Lord to please help me.

The Lord spoke, "I have always been with you. My people know my Word and hear for only now you have received the Word and believe thee. First pull your net on board."

"Please help me," I asked once more. As my hand touched His robe, I felt virtue come into my soul.

We pulled the net on board, and the Lord spoke through the fire and said, "You have been pulled by this net."

As the great white ship rocked and was tossed about, we pulled it out of the sea of sin.

The Lord said, "Let's see what thee has caught."

I looked down into the net and saw my soul, for the Lord had helped me pull and save my soul—had saved me—from this world of sin.

As we looked into the net, the Lord said, "I still do miracles."

* * *

A man that I met has touched my soul. He spoke; his voice was like the golden sweet oil of sugarcane. I could not see him as I would you in the natural, but His presence was known to me in the spirit and soul. He had a great sense of stillness, for all movements about Him were smooth and not of torment. I could see his form, although it was like a glimpse of wind, like that of a butterfly that was unnatural. He had come to give me faith and to clean my soul of unholy ways to humble me in all things; by this I could only receive the knowledge of the Word. As a newborn innocent, I am now one who belongs to the Lord thy God. Such shall I be called the Nazirite for He is strong in the Word.

* * *

Today I went to the bus stop.

Once on the bus I asked the driver, "Please take me anywhere."

"That will cost a great deal," the driver said. "Because there is no destination."

"Then there would be no cost," I said in return.

To my surprise the driver said, "To one that has no destination, there is a great price to pay for he is lost."

Then as the driver turned to me, I saw that He was the Lord thy God. For one that is lost, the price of the destination is hell on earth and damnation.

"What must I do?" I asked. "For I am weary and have had no place of rest."

The Lord said, “Come and lay your burdens and cares on me for I am one that would give you rest in a place and peace of soul in your heart.”

I begged, “Please help, oh Lord.”

And the Lord said, “That is all you had to say. I have been here during your life’s journey.”

* * *

This man had a key, and it was made of gold and silver. He did not have any idea what it really was, but once I saw it, I remembered it was the key to heaven and hell that Christ had. So, I followed this man everywhere he went. Each time he stopped, he turned and looked around to see if anyone was looking before he used the key. For this key would open any door within our universe. It was used by someone who had no faith, direction in life, or purpose. Each time I saw him use it, I waited for the right moment to obtain it. My purpose was to use it for one reason, which was to get into the gates of heaven.

* * *

I came to a crossroad that had many signs and directions about which way to go. Because I was lost and had many burdens, I paused and wondered which was the best road to travel. For in my heart, I did not know which direction to go. I had wasted my life’s journey.

I noticed a man coming toward me. He, too, was looking at the signs. He said, “All times and distance are not worth the road that you choose, for I will give thee the quickest road for your rest.”

I said, “Can’t be!”

He said "Yes, have faith, be humbled, and you're there, for heaven is where this road will take you."

* * *

I entered the library wanting to find a book on how to be rich and famous because I had nothing. I noticed a librarian, so I walked over and asked her for help. She said she had just the book that I needed. I was taken down a long row, which had over 10,000 books. She stopped and pointed up to a certain book for me to take from the shelf. She told me this book would have all the knowledge I needed to obtain all my life's riches. Once I pulled the book down, I noticed it was the Bible. I looked at her and said this is the wrong book for this cannot help me. Then she took me down another long row of books. A book that had golden leaves on the end of it stuck out more than all the others for it was so beautiful. Once I pulled it off the shelf, it was the same book: the Bible. I told her instantly there is no way this book can help me. She said this book will give me all my life's riches and save my soul, plus there was no deposit or return.

Minister Byron Hodges is a prophetic poet and dreamer. He is a graduate of Agape School of Ministry. He also majored in Western Civilization at the University of Arkansas at Little Rock. Married To author Phyllis Hodges for 47 years, they have two adult children and three young adult grandchildren. His first book will be published in 2022.

My Pandemic Journey

BY PHYLLIS HODGES

My personal pandemic journey began March 13, 2020. During this unprecedented time, there were many new events for my family and me.

I received favor, which was more than I ever expected. There was help in so many areas during this world crisis. For the first time in my life, I experienced food banks and drive-thru assistance. I received help with my utilities and mortgage. I witnessed things that I never dreamed I'd see. People were all over the place, in long lines waiting and communicating with each other, both inside and outside of their vehicles.

Due to the shutdown, my husband and our adult children heard a lot about the quarantine. People were getting sick or exposed to the virus, and they were given instructions on how to quarantine. I spent a lot of special time providing evening and nighttime drives with my mom. This was much needed by both of us because we were always super close AKA best friends, but this even made us closer. Mom was in the age bracket that was critical during this health crisis.

My family chose not to have her out at various places or do anything on her own. We made sure she had all the necessary items and food in her home, so there was no need for her to leave the confinement of her home.

There were special things that were accomplished during this season of my life: I learned and created new Zoom, live, and streaming projects. I was blessed to be featured in a special on Channel 4 News during Women's History month. The producers came to my home to record the show, and we had so much fun socializing. I also attended numerous online workshops and various trainings because no one was doing any in-person gathering.

The pandemic caused everything to close including churches, schools, businesses, government offices, public parks, and facilities. There were travel bans on various cities. Everyone was required to wear masks, gloves, and wash their hands frequently. People were also asked to practice social distancing while following the CDC guidelines. Most folks followed those guidelines but not all.

There were no places to go to feel safe and no places to go to dress up, therefore I created an event called Plantation Tea Parties. This event turned into a movement to celebrate women. Everyone was excited to finally have an opportunity to dress up. The fear factor was not there when it came to this event because it was going to be held outside. My property was so large that we could automatically socially distance without trying. We dressed up in our finest outfits, wore fancy gloves, and the invitation was for ten guests only, per each tea party. This event was such a success, people started reserving seats for the next Plantation Tea Parties.

Another new experience for my hubby and me was our online church service. Due to churches being closed, technology was what we all turned to. The uniqueness of this process was that we had the opportunity to enjoy and engage in more services during the day. We made a conscious decision to get up and get dressed as if we were going to a regular in-person church service. This was done so that we were able to enjoy praise and worship, the Word, and giving online. And it was our way of still honoring God while adjusting to a new way of having church.

Something else that I found enjoyable was riding around looking for homeless people. We prepared nonperishable foods and gathered plenty of clothing for the people in need. This made us happy to be able to bless others in need.

During the pandemic, I created things I had never made before and enjoyed some things I would normally take for granted. I spent more time outside. My form of decorating went to another level—literally from the front of the property line to the end of it. I planted flowers, fruits, and veggies. I had an eye for color, and I wanted a new look all around due to us being at home all the time. I desired to see new things, so I decided to paint everything I saw including the deck, outside furniture, yard art, etc. You name it, I painted it.

One day I received a phone call and an invitation from my sister regarding a trip that she and our mom were going to take. She asked if I was interested in taking a girls trip. I replied, "In this pandemic?"

I laughed, and I think I was about to become delirious and hysterical. I do not know what it was I was feeling, but I agreed to go. A few-days getaway to Texas would do my soul some good. This trip was our first and only trip during the long pandemic.

Once I returned, I spent several days climbing mountains with my hubby getting slate rocks and creating more art.

The pandemic changed my lifestyle tremendously. All my fitness centers were closed effective March 13, 2020, and all of the nursing homes that I provided fitness services to were also closed to everyone with the exception of doctors and nurses. So, what did that mean? No money coming into the Hodges household from me.

It was extremely hard to get unemployment started since the crisis was so new to everyone. It became frustrating and challenging because it seemed everyone had different answers on ways to get help for those in need, but their ways did not work. Finally, the kinks were worked out and the Pandemic Unemployment Assistance (PUA) started.

Politics also played a serious role during that time. There seemed to be a major uprise in hatred and racism, as if we the people were going backwards. We lost so many African American men for unjust reasons.

Congressman John Lewis fought a good fight against cancer during these unrestful times. Trump was finally out of the White House, and we made history as a nation. We elected Kamala Harris, the first woman and first Black and Asian American, as Vice President of the United States of America. The 46th President, Joe Biden, came in assisting Americans with a stimulus package of $1400, one of many ways he aided people in need.

COVID-19 was cruel to many people. My husband and I personally lost at least five people that we loved and knew well to this horrible nightmare. Our family was also attacked. Our youngest granddaughter caught COVID-19 while away serving in the military. The most devastating part was that she caught a second bout with it less than sixty days apart. Unfortunately, the CDC, the government officials, and the world were not talking about the second bout. This horrific attack on humans was so unknown, it was not initially clear that you could contract this illness again.

As I write and reflect, it is June 2021. Therefore, a year and three months have passed, and schools, churches, restaurants, various city facilities, and job sites are slowly opening back up. At this time, people are still unpredictable with their thought processes, which is confusing because the virus is still alive and well, but our state (and so many others) has lifted the ban of wearing masks.

I have had a lot of pain during this pandemic. In addition to losing friends, I lost my best friend, my brother James, in April during this crisis. Unfortunately, he passed but it was not COVID-related.

During the Arkansas snowstorm, I also slipped on some black ice and broke my ankle in three parts. I had an emergency surgery; two plates and thirteen pins were added to my ankle to repair it.

But I have also had a lot of joy during this season of my life, too. Blessed to see another year, I am now 63. I wrote a book titled *Girl Power* and am currently working on another book, which will be out later this year. I also had the opportunity to participate in the virtual audience of a variety of television shows: *Wendy Williams, Dr. Phil, Tamron Hall, The View,* and *America's Funniest Home Videos.* Now that was unique and super fun.

This all made me realize there is nothing too hard for God to help you through, even if it's a pandemic.

Phyllis Hodges, CFT, LHM is considered a serial entrepreneur due to her many successful business ventures. As clergy, one of her biggest highlights was being the owner of from 2000-2019 of Carousel Fit 4 Life Wellness Center, a faith-based wellness and fitness center, which was located in the historic district of

Argenta, North Little Rock Arkansas. As a fitness specialist, she travels and implements fitness programs for individuals and corporations internationally. Phyllis is also a best-selling author of several books: A Devine Connection, a fitness motivational book; 8 Years of Unforgettable History, a living history book with the location highlights of the Little Rock Governor's Mansion Library, the FBI Library in Quantico, Virginia, and the Arkansas National Guard Museum at the Camp Robinson base in North Little Rock, Arkansas; and Girl Power, a nonfiction compilation book. She also written two short stories, which were included in The Writing Our Lives Anthology, Volumes II & III; School Days, A Reflection of My Living History. Her focus now is to team up with her husband, author and Minister Byron, who is a prophetic poet and dreamer. They have been married 47 years with two adult children and three young adult grandchildren. She can be contacted on her website doyouphylme.com, all social media outlets, and her live productions titled "Celebrate," "Book Talk," and "The Hodges," which are streaming live on Facebook, Zoom, Instagram, and YouTube.

I Just Want to Live

BY JANET HOLMES UCHENDU

It is Monday, December 28, 2020, 8 p.m. My daughter, Janetta, has just informed me and her father, Ogugua, that she has tested positive for COVID-19. She continues to speak. Her mouth is moving, but why so slowly? Why is there no sound? What is this rapid-fire drumbeat? It is so loud. I watch my husband's and daughter's faces. Do they not hear the drum?

Okay, okay, calm down. Must regain control. Must not alarm them. Sound returns and I am hearing words with which I am agreeing. We live in the same household, so husband and I must get tested, too.

The following day, Tuesday, December 29, we get tested. Ours is not a rapid test, so we don't learn our results until the next day, Wednesday, December 30.

Positive!

Both my husband and I test positive. But how did this happen? We have been so careful. We have been hyper-vigilant. How did this happen? Think! Does it matter how? The fact is we have tested positive.

* * *

On Friday, March 13, 2020, I was instructed to take my laptop home with me at the end of the workday, and I was told not to return to the building until further notice. Two days prior to this on Wednesday, March 11, 2020, the World Health Organization (WHO) had declared COVID-19 a pandemic. The director general of WHO said at a briefing in Geneva, the agency is "deeply concerned by the alarming levels of spread and severity" of the outbreak.

Also, on Friday, March 13, 2020, President Donald J. Trump, declared the novel coronavirus a national emergency, and the Trump administration issued a travel ban on non-Americans who visited twenty-six European countries within fourteen days of coming to the United States. Side note: People traveling from the United Kingdom and the Republic of Ireland were exempt.

I was oblivious to all of this on March 13, 2020, realizing much later that due to recent changes that had been implemented at my place of employment, I could have very easily been exposed to this new virus.

I held my breath, prayed, and bided my time. I was so relieved when as time passed, I didn't get sick. I felt like I had not contracted the virus and was in the clear.

I went into a hyper-vigilant state of existence. I continued to work from home and did not venture out of my home to stores or restaurants. My husband and daughter both worked in fields where they were considered essential workers, so daily they had to venture out into the world. We had frequent conversations about the fact that they also needed to be hyper-vigilant because they could bring the virus home to me. We made masks for ourselves, googling to find the best material to use. As the pandemic worsened, we also made masks for family and friends.

* * *

By June 2020, I was no longer employed. Being home and having a clear understanding with my husband and daughter of their need to be careful, I felt relatively safe. I watched the daily news. I only ventured out occasionally, mostly to the library to pick up or return books using their no contact system, and I, too, was cautious.

Whenever I ventured out, I wore my mask. I washed my hands and used sanitizer when I left home and returned. I had sanitizer in my car and in my purse. When there was an Amazon delivery, I would mask up before opening the door. Eventually I stopped opening the door. Instead, I would wait until the delivery was completed, then I would spray the package with Lysol or Microban, wait for it to dry, then bring it inside.

* * *

On that fateful Monday morning, December 28, Janetta told me she didn't feel well, so she was not going to work, and she said that later she was going to get tested for COVID-19.

By Wednesday, December 30, I was in survival mode. I tried not to focus on the fact that we were in the holiday season, Christmas and the New Year. I tried to keep at bay the unsettling thought that we might die. I had been consuming the news, so I prayed that we would not end up in the hospital. To me, that was a death sentence.

We called and called but could not get in to see a doctor, and we quickly became sicker and sicker each day.

We spoke with family and friends, and yes, we googled to learn everything we could. One friend knew people in the medical field. She sent me a long list of over-the-counter medications to take, liquids to consume, and instructions to follow in our quest to survive COVID-19. Another friend ordered all the medications online and had them delivered to our home. Our daughter, Bridget, made a major grocery run, and a good family friend made runs for fast food and Ensure.

Within a few days of testing positive for COVID-19, Ogugua and I lost our sense of smell and taste. Janetta did not. We grew weak; we had trouble breathing, especially at night; we could not walk from our bedrooms down the hallway to the kitchen without leaning on and sliding along the wall for support, and those were just some of our issues. We each lost about 25 pounds, and while Janetta and I were okay with that, Ogugua didn't have 25 pounds to spare. Of the three of us, he became the sickest. At night I watched him as he slept, making sure he was still breathing.

We drank so much Gatorade and ate so much chicken soup, that it will be okay with me if I never "need" to consume these two particular foods ever again in my lifetime.

* * *

We contracted the virus before the vaccine was available. We are now fully vaccinated and plan to get booster shots as soon as we are eligible.

We continue to deal with COVID-19 long-hauler symptoms, which, at first, we didn't talk about with each other because our symptoms were varied, hard to describe, and sometimes caused us to question our sanity. For a while, we experienced shortness of breath while just sitting. I continue to have difficulty concentrating, and reading is a challenge.

Ogugua and I regained our sense of taste in stages. For many months, foods didn't taste like they did before we had the virus. We both have partially regained our sense of smell.

I understand COVID-19 experiences are far from cookie-cutter. For Janetta, Ogugua, and me, battling COVID-19 was an ordeal. There has been but one other time in my life when I have prayed so fervently.

Lord, let us live. I just want to live.

My prayer was heard. By the grace of God, we are still here.

Janet Holmes Uchendu is a first-year graduate student at the University of Arkansas at Conway (UCA) pursuing her MFA in Creative Writing. She has a B.A. in Music Education from Philander Smith College in Little Rock, Arkansas. She worked seventeen years in the commercial insurance industry, and prior to leaving the workforce in June 2020, she spent twelve years working in the non-profit sector. She took her first writing course, Introduction to Creative Writing, in April 2018, at UCA.

Arkansas, Home away from Home

BY FELIX KARIUKI

The first time I stepped into Little Rock, Arkansas, the experience was both exciting and confusing. I had connected my flight through Dallas Fort Worth International Airport, and the contrast between Dallas and Little Rock, my first two US cities, was resounding. From big spacious buildings, big planes, and an ocean of humanity, to a tiny airport with fewer scattered, smaller jets, and arrivals as main occupants.

Prior to my arrival, my perception of America had been a byproduct of what I had seen on TV, movies, and stories I'd heard from those who once lived in the country and had relocated back home. Anything big, luxurious, and seemingly out of this world, was the America I knew and expected.

My host picked me up on time, and as we drove down on the slender, broken tarmac of what was known as Asher Avenue, my confusion only worsened. Marking each side of the road were spots of dilapidated wooden buildings with broken windows. A site that I could only reference to two settings in Kenya, rural or a slum (i.e., an informal settlement in a city).

Were it not for my host, I would have confidently declared myself lost in search of America.

The days that followed as I settled in corresponded to a musical chair dance, with me often missing a seat. My first cultural experience in school was wondering how to respond when someone says, "What's up?"

Never in my life had I ever been made aware of such a greeting. It had neither been featured in the twelve years of British English classes I took nor in any of the extra English content I consumed.

Should I answer with, "the sky or the roof"?

On a few occasions I did give them as answers, until my speech class lecturer pointed out the need to be kind in my response.

Twelve years in a British schooling system ideally had honed my English to perfection. My first visit to a McDonalds on a hot summer afternoon, however, made me question if indeed I could speak the language. Having confidently walked to the counter, I was asked, in all kindness, if my order was for there or to go. Being a proclaimed master of the language with certificates to show for it, I simply belted, "A takeaway."

"Say who?"

"A takeaway."

It was then that I knew my English classes had been a waste of money, and I justifiably needed my refund from each institution.

I had taken English as a subject. "Who" in the Queen's language typically referenced a person, not an item. This was the United States of America, a country whose Constitution reflected on the use of English as the language of communication. Wouldn't its citizens be better masters of the language than someone who was a beneficiary of a past colonial system? Though I did eventually get a "to go" meal, the experience did highlight the society's gap for an effective literacy program.

All residents of former British colonies in the south-to-south countries have a habit of dressing to impress at all formal environments, including institutes of higher learning. On a normal working day, a distinguishing mark that you are employed or function in an environment that drives the country's economy would be the inclusion of a suit jacket as part of your attire. It is on this premise that on my first day of summer school, I attended a morning class dressed in a complete suit and tie, only to observe my classmates walking into class in what I assumed were pajamas.

The site of women smoking freely was a marker of how far removed I was from Africa, let alone Kenya. The physical distance between the US and Africa seemed to be directly proportional to the social and economic distance between the two. The definition of gender equity between the two environments compared to pitying entities that lived on land and those that lived in water. The two were different. Women in the US apparently seemed freer compared to women in Africa, who still bore the heavier burden of a patriarchal society.

Coming from Kenya, divorces were rare at the time. Once joined in holy matrimony, couples would ride together until the wheels came off; they would change the tires and keep at it. In the US, however, marriage seemed to have a different connotation. The number of times I was introduced to exes made me question the institution's validity as the cell unit of a human society.

Tougher, though, in my judgment, was and still is Africa's legalized tradition, polygamy. All else pales in light of it. I know of a man at the age of 38-years-old, who had legally married seventeen women and sired thirty-two children with a goal of beating his dad's record of having sixty-nine wives and 140 children. For each, he had provided comfortable living a stone's throw away from each other and good livelihoods. Weekly, the wives with protocols based on seniority would hold a meeting to address all economic, social, and environmental matters pertaining to their husband's interests, chaired by the "Man" himself or the senior-most wife present.

In Africa, anytime someone invites you out, the tradition is that all expenses associated with the outing fall squarely on the shoulders of the one who extended the invitation.

My first night out in Little Rock, however, was a lesson to be retained. Seated with friends, a plan formed to take an out-of-town guest to dinner. As a student conscious of my financial limits, I opted to stay behind. This, however, did not sit too well with the group, so they peer-pressured me. As a newbie to the culture, I gave in.

Having selected a nearby Chinese restaurant, we all gleefully trooped for a night of celebration. After hours of talks and laughter, bill time came. Without missing a beat, the server had separated the bills with each perfectly attached to its owner. It was then that I quickly learned the art of saying "no" to invitations that had financial consequences.

During the summer, I had been given the option of taking only one course, if any. Being studious and eager to get courses knocked out, I had chosen one: Speech Communication. But the campus that summer felt empty. There was hardly anyone in sight.

The Fall semester on campus, however, was nothing but a joy; day one was a beehive. The campus was bursting with activities. Never had I seen so many American students in one place. It felt like a scene from a movie, only that I was actually living it. Hallways were filled with excitement. Girls dressed to kill and boys the same. Fraternity and sorority groups looking for a recruit to pounce on as they rendered the air with their signature calls could be seen at every corner. For the first time, this felt like America.

Earlier, before my fall semester, I had been introduced to a group of African students, who frequently met to share laughter and stories of their experiences in the newfoundland over some African delicacy and music that reminded them of home. The group representative of each geographic region in Africa proved to be supportive. Through their support, I had been able to integrate into the American system, including quickly and seamlessly joining a church. I must confess that the churches in Little Rock came as another surprise to me. Up until then, nothing had been indicative of such an existence.

Eager to see a church one Sunday morning, I requested to be picked up and taken to one.

If heaven was St. Mark Baptist Church, then I had made it there. If divinity had been a fable, then I had just become a believer. If angels do walk on earth, then I was among them. Saying the atmosphere was ignited would be insufficient. It was lit. Supercharged. Stratospherically on fire. I wondered, *Where have you all been?*

Ever found yourself shaking to a beat as if you already knew it? Something about the sound of the drums took me home. I could hear the rhythm somewhere deep within. There was a connection. My legs were popping. Suddenly

I couldn't feel the ground. I was in my element; I was home free.

In Kenya, locating a Christian was easy. They walked branded, "I am saved." You could easily spot one anywhere.

Stepping into church on this particular Sunday morning had been the bread my soul needed. As the beats played and the word broke into palatable pieces, it was clear that spiritually I was famished.

One of the classes I had registered for that fall was Composition 1. I had debated skipping it and registering for Composition 2 at the advice of a friend, who had taken a similar class. This, however, was deemed not possible by my official academic advisor, who adamantly insisted on following the usual protocol. And so, complying, I found myself attending a class I could easily have served as a substitute teacher. It was in this class, though, that the bell of purpose rang loudly, beckoning to a life of reason.

One evening, the lecturer decided to jolt our senses with a unique assignment: "Tonight, I would like each one of you to write your own obituary. Who knows what an obituary is?"

We all knew what it was. You could tell from the laughter that ensued when someone echoed, "Say who?"

Raw and sincere it was. Not too many people are conscious or want to be aware that everyone is on borrowed time. That every minute gone is a subtraction to one's time on planet Earth, and hence, carries a bankable value that ought to be well-spent and that will be evidenced by the narrative others will be tasked to give of one's life.

As a man born oceans away, my days were filled with questions triggered by my voice. I had an accent, though not as heavy as my brothers from West Africa, which lacked the signatory southern drawl. My sentences seemed to be well-spaced, punctuated, and "proper." So often I was asked where I came from or where I learned to speak such good English.

I would joke around, depending on who I was talking to, and include tales of the "jungle" as depicted in certain movies. At times, though, I would take my time to feed a sincerely curious mind, conscious of the fact that I could have been the needed link for further exploration of life outside the US of places such as Lake Turkana, the "Jaded Sea," that derived its name from its characteristic nature of changing colors and where the oldest remains of humans, 3.5 million-years-old, were found.

In retrospect, it was interesting how many hats I wore in a day representing governments, and every institute, and person on the continent of Africa. I was surprised that most people I met knew of Africa as a country and former President Nelson Mandela as its president, with no hint that Africa was actually a continent made up of fifty-five independent governments and a population that spoke more than 2000 languages.

In Kenya, Christmas and Easter holidays are the most celebrated public Christian holidays, with Christmas topping the list. Most people, young and old, live for its festivities. With schools closed, most families usually schedule their vacations around Christmas. Consequently, on the day of celebration, roads leading away from the capital city, Nairobi, are usually backed up by heavy traffic all morning.

Thanksgiving, arguably equally the most celebrated American holiday, was new to me. Never had I tasted turkey before. I had, however, heard of the turkey dinner nap theory, where everyone falls asleep after eating turkey, reminiscent of a scene from *Zombieland*, where everyone woke up afterward and got ready for Black Friday sales.

Seeking induction into this American tradition, on my first Thanksgiving holiday I chose to accompany some of my student friends, who had planned to have a Thanksgiving dinner at a ranch outside Little Rock. The visit proved to be more than a bargain. Not only was I able to verify the effect of tryptophan from turkey consumption, which induces serotonin in the brain and causes sleep, but, for the first time, when we all sat outside around a campfire with marshmallow sticks in our hands, I saw stars in the southern sky. For a moment, I sensed how interconnected and equal humans are as the same sky stood above all.

One thing I cannot fail to mention is my encounter with US police officers. America is blessed. The discipline held by each I encountered was enviable. The kindness exerted, unbelievable. The relationship I saw on campus between police officers and students was pleasantly surprising. Never had I witnessed such a peaceful coexistence between the two.

At the time, in the country I was coming from, students were known to riot and protest frequently, and police officers were known for being unfriendly. A student, therefore, typically would never be seen asking for directions from a police officer. You would not find the two sharing a laugh. It was a constant cat and mouse chase, the cartoon character Jerry always running away from Tom.

Felix Kimani Kariuki is a registered engineer. He currently lives in Kenya but lived in Little Rock, Arkansas, for 17 years. He serves as the Programmes Director at Programme for Capacity Development in Africa, P4CDA, https://p4cda.net, which is the Global Open Data for Agriculture and Nutrition's (GODAN's) Africa secretariat, https://godan.info. In this role, he works with governments, academia, nonprofit organizations, farmer associations, and the private sector in creating and promoting open data platforms that will strengthen South to South cooperation and triangular collaboration as a means for building capacity, technology transfer and knowledge sharing to enable collective effort in addressing challenges of data gaps in food nutrition and security. He is also the Director of Africa Online Learning at Ycenter, headquartered in New York City.

My Arkansas and the Deep South: Still Reliving our History

BY JANETTA KEARNEY

I grew up in the pre-civil rights era in a southeast Arkansas Delta. While I experienced social and racial injustices, I was always taught that things were changing for the better, and if we gave it time and did our part, America would get it right.

I have spent the last year reflecting on where we are as a country. I was not prepared for the daily stories and images that showed us in black and white, the level of racial and social disparities still so much a part of our country. Like so many others, I was hopeful that we were going in the right direction. It took a global pandemic to show us how far we are from that dream.

What I've realized is that, in spite of all the invaluable lessons learned from growing up in my small Arkansas community, all the hope our parents and teachers tried to ingrain in us, they—our parents and teachers—would not recognize the America we are today.

I know I speak for millions when I say we are all in need of universal PTSD therapy. It has been almost two years of continuous pain and anger as the stories continue to get worse. Not only the seemingly endless deaths from the COVID-19 pandemic but the endless killing of Black Americans by police. While the media highlighted the deaths of George Floyd, Breonna Taylor, and Ahmaud Arbery, there are actually too many deaths to mention.

And, then there were a former president's efforts to change the Constitution and deny a presidential election; and some states took laws into their own hands to turn back equal rights for women, deny voting rights for Black, Brown and young people; and the overall campaign to minimize and devalue Black Americans, especially in the southern states.

It will take years to rebuild the communities that the COVID-19 pandemic destroyed. Beyond the 700,000 COVID-related deaths is the stark realization that little has changed throughout our country, including who benefits from the institutions that were put in place to make life better for *all* Americans such as healthcare, education, the judicial, public safety, and our economic systems.

It was made abundantly clear that the COVID pandemic disproportionately impacted families and children of Black and Brown families. But, to make matters worse, safety net programs ended up benefitting the rich far more than it did those in dire need. Another glaring example of social injustices based on race and economic need.

For years, I have implored decision makers and community leaders to sit down and talk about the problems in hopes of finding ways to fix at least some of them. The first step, I'm finding, is getting leaders to admit there are problems. Too many are still denying that race is at the root of so many of these atrocities. The facts and numbers don't lie.

As I reflect on where we are as a country, I'm remembering the place I grew up in, the southeast Arkansas Delta. Yes, I was taught to pray, work, and believe in a better tomorrow, but I can also see that some of the same issues our leaders refuse to address today were the problems we experienced then—the overwhelming educational, social and economic injustices. These are all issues that we as a community and a state must address. And we must all roll up our sleeves to do the hard work if we care about our children and their future.

As a child, I witnessed racial, gender and color discrimination, even when I didn't fully understand how deeply ingrained and pervasive that discrimination was throughout America. Though it was there all around us, it was more subtle, and in reality, racism and discrimination was accepted as simply, "That's just the way things are." Even then, though, I felt that discrimination—whether subtle or overt—was imbalanced and hurtful. As my perception grew, it became evident that Whites in particular, but also some emotionally or mentally scarred Blacks, participated in promoting racial inequality, even though, to be fair, they often believed they were protecting us, teaching us to stay in "our place," and to not upset the apple cart.

One hard lesson about racism was learning that my, and other Black children's, worth were based on how light our skin was. There were a lot of children in my family, and we were not the same in any way. A few of us were what others called light-skinned, some "paper sack" brown, and others a shade darker. I was one of my parents' dark-brown children. Imagine learning that others graded our worth based on our skin color. That was one more strike against a Black child.

I didn't know it then, but I soon learned that the grandparents or great-grandparents of the lighter-complexioned Blacks were most often children of White slaveowners. The innocent female slaves were involuntarily impregnated by the slaveowners—often through rape. Yet, in spite of the horrific reason behind the lighter-colored children, they were considered socially superior to the pure, unmixed Blacks because their color was closer to Whites.

This has led to decades of color prejudice by both Blacks and Whites. During the infamous Jim Crow era, the "paper-bag test" was used by both Blacks and Whites to discern Blacks' acceptability. Only those who were as light or lighter than a brown paper bag was considered socially acceptable. That is how insane racial and color prejudice is, and sadly, how deeply it has been ingrained into our own culture. What is saddest is that this has not completely disappeared from our culture.

Unfortunately, it wasn't just in our homes or in interactions with Whites that I experienced racial prejudice. In fact, I learned of the devaluation of our worth from my Sunday school, church, and our all-Black public school. It was pervasive throughout our surroundings. This was *so* pervasive and troubling that by the time I was in my young teen years, I had already decided I would leave the Arkansas Delta.

I was an avid reader, and thankfully my parents always made sure there were books and magazines in our home. Thanks to the stories and articles I read, I dreamed of a different kind of world and of moving away and living a life much like the ones I read about in those books and magazines.

I graduated from Fields High School at 17, and as my siblings before me, I left home to attend college that next fall. I enrolled into Arkansas Agricultural Mechanical and Normal College (AM&N), an HBCU in Pine Bluff,

Arkansas. I was excited to be leaving home and for the independence that meant. It was my first step into maturity and away from parental controls and the don'ts of Sunday school and church. I took my parents' ideals with me, however. They'd always taught us we could be anything we wanted to be if we prepared for it and if we kept God in our lives. They also encouraged us to find a way to give back, saying that it would result in a happier, more productive life.

My excitement about college soon came to a screeching halt. Once again, I was confronted with racism, inequality, and colorism within the four walls of my college. I was reminded that I should "stay in your place" and not aspire to something that is reserved for Whites.

When I proudly told the admissions officer I was interested in studying, "Journalism, newspaper reporting, or writing…like Edward R Murrow," there was first a look of disbelief on the registrars' faces followed immediately by derisive laughter as if they were wondering, "Who is this colored girl daring to believe she could be something no other Black student had aspired to?"

I was embarrassed and hurt even more when they called me names my parents had forbidden us to ever use—names I thought that only Whites used against Blacks. One of the women looked at me, and asked, "Do you know you're a n…, who do you think you are?"

This was a perfect example of how adults—Black and White—deny young Blacks' intelligence and devalue their pain and emotional abuse. Sadly, this pain is embedded in children's subconscious, and it sometimes takes years of hard work through conversation to right this wrong.

Many years later, I learned about the Willie Lynch letter and its connection to the power of dismissive, hurtful responses. The power of the Lynch letter was that it outlined ways White farmers could effectively control Blacks and slaves and maintain the foundation of slavery, even when and if the Congressional laws changed.

We only have to review what has happened over the last two years to realize that the indoctrination was strong, effective and continues to live even today in the South and especially in Arkansas' Delta region. Those who dare raise their voices in efforts to uplift the poor and bring programs to the community that will help youth learn new skills, grow, and become their best selves are too often shut down or ignored, destroying the message and muting the messenger. I know. I was one of those voices threatened.

There has been a long list of historical racial events that bear out this truth. Not only in the South, but in Arkansas. Two such events were the Elaine Race Riot of 1919, where hundreds of Blacks were killed after veterans and others from the area returned and advocated fair prices for crops and work; there was also the Tulsa Massacre of 1921, where hundreds of Blacks were killed, and Tulsa's Black Wall Street was destroyed. To date, the only economic reparations for loss was made to the White community, not the victimized Black one.

I have my own personal list of race and gender-related experiences, times I tried to create change for our state, communities, and children. They include my efforts to make a difference in my hometown of Gould in Lincoln County and in my role as publisher of the *Arkansas State Press* newspaper, when I dared question how three Black men shot in the back by police were a justifiable threat to police. Just shortly after I wrote that editorial, I was arrested, and police took me to jail. A Little Rock Sherriff insisted, however, that I not be kept there.

Some years later, I applied for and was awarded a federally-funded education grant that I hoped to use for a youth education program in my hometown of Gould. But my efforts were rebuffed by the town itself. This included Gould's mayor declaring that I was unlike my siblings, as if we should all act, talk, and accept the same. This demand that all Blacks act and react alike has been used against African Americans since 1619 when Africans were forced to America as chattel.

Realizing I needed an emotional and spiritual break after the onslaught of unfair and unjust encounters, I left Arkansas. This was one of the best decisions I could have made. In fact, it may have saved my life. In another state that was more accepting of diversity and multiculturalism, my sense of self and emotional awareness grew. In my new state, acceptability was based on ethics, conversations, and contributions without regard to one's race. In this racially-diverse environment, the comfort level in sharing history and professional development were like emotional sunshine. Open dialogue about life built confidence.

In spite of all I have experienced, I remain an eternal optimist. My most recent return to Arkansas came with the hope to help the state move forward. Our parents implored us to, "Find a way to make the world a better place," and I am fully prepared to do exactly that. I am more than willing to share my knowledge, experience, skills, triumphs, and trials. I am also eager to help educators offer open learning for youth who, like me, grew up not being exposed to much beyond family and community. I know this can increase critical thinking.

While I am still experiencing negative attitudes from my efforts, I continue to fight the uphill battle of trying to open conversations about the things that keep us at the bottom of every social and educational measurement.

Arkansas cannot progress until our leaders accept and admit the fact that many of the racist policies in place before the civil rights laws were passed are still alive and well. Our children and our communities are suffering because of this.

I am just one person, but I feel a responsibility to do all I can do. That is the legacy left to me by two amazing parents, who did their all to send their seventeen children out into the world to make a difference. I am their most stubborn child, and I wear that badge and their legacy with pride.

Janetta Kearney is an experienced lawyer and mediator-negotiator. She combines her skills with her knowledge of laws and policies to facilitate resolutions, policies, and decisions, all designed to be more equitable than "best practices." She believes education—formal or zip code observances and experiences—is the basis of understanding. She says the US Constitution contradicts itself by noting that, "All men are created equal" but later stating "forced [African and their descendants] slaves [mankind] are 3/5 of a man." She is dedicated to determining how we teach, learn, and live with those basic life contradictions.

Surrounded By It

BY RENEE' LA VINESS

In the middle of the night, my husband raced through the living room, stopped abruptly at the space heater, and turned it all the way up. He dropped into a sitting position in front of it and shook violently due to a scary high fever. I put him to bed and wiped his face, neck, and chest with a cool wet rag, trying to lower his temperature. Three hours later, the fever disappeared, but he stayed home from work for the next five days, due to not feeling well.

We avoided each other for weeks after that. Although always shared a kiss or hug every time we parted or reunited, something felt scary about this illness.

A few weeks later, on a nice day in March, my nose ran and my eyes poured constant streams down my cheeks. The night before, I woke with a start, unable to fill my lungs with air. I wanted to believe I had psychosomatically caused my own symptoms after hearing the Coronavirus was finally in the United States. Shortness of breath was one of the main symptoms. Runny nose and eyes were not on the list.

"Allergies," my friend said. "You've got allergies."

"That's not normal for me though," I told her. "I don't have allergies that do *this*."

"Maybe you've got that China Virus. They say it's made it to America, you know."

True. The news announced it was in the coastal states over the past few days, but it shouldn't have arrived in Oklahoma yet.

The day after my nose and eyes cleared up, my throat stung like I had swallowed a sticktight and it was stuck tight to the back of my throat. No amount of coughing, swallowing, water, cough drops, or allergy medicine made it better. Thankfully, that lasted less than twenty-four hours.

Some friends were having similar symptoms. Everyone called it "allergies." Since I'd never had allergies, I was an easy sell. Must be part of aging. Although irritating, most of the stuff had been endurable.

Someone was diagnosed with the flu. Maybe I had it, too. I decided to stay home. I missed critique meetings, didn't volunteer at the school library, didn't go see the grandkids, and didn't visit my elderly mother.

Dry eyes were next. The dryness hurt way behind my eyes. After that calmed down, I thought I was done with whatever I'd had. So, I stayed up all night and worked on editing and writing projects.

The next day, I slept, waking only long enough to visit the bathroom, but I didn't care to eat and had to be reminded to take my blood pressure medicine. Assuming the sickness had worn me out, I allowed my body to rest.

After two days of sleep, I was wide awake and working again. It didn't last, though. When I sat at my computer for only a few minutes, my backbone threatened to collapse. For some reason, it was not strong enough to hold me upright. I rushed toward the bedroom, barely landing on the bed before my body gave out.

Everyone said I should get tested. I called the hotline. There were only two people in Oklahoma who were known to have it, and they were being quarantined. The lady on the phone asked if I had been anywhere those two people had been. I assured her that, if I knew who they were and where they'd been, I could say for sure.

"Exactly," she snarked. In other words, if I didn't know who they were, I must not have been where they had been, so I couldn't have it.

Then came the hard, dry cough. No big deal. Like everything else, it lasted only a couple of days.

The wet cough followed and almost turned into pneumonia. I worked hard to prevent the drainage from reaching my lungs. I learned to cough immediately when I felt the tickle in my throat. If I inhaled first, like normal, I could not cough it out.

After surviving the wet cough, two or more weeks had gone by. The "flu" had never lasted so long.

After no symptoms for a full week, I returned to my volunteer work at the school library. The other volunteer had not come in for a few days, because she was sick. So I took special care cleaning around her desk and anywhere she or I might touch. I enjoyed being with the kids again.

When school let out, I walked home. The sun was shining, and the day wasn't too hot or cold. About halfway there, one of the neighbor kids waved at me from across the street. It was nice to be recognized after school.

Seconds later, my legs felt as if someone had filled them with wet cement. They did not want to move. This was different than the flu aches, and it affected only my legs. I was little more than three houses from home and afraid I couldn't walk that far.

I called my husband, hoping he would pick me up on his way, but he wasn't going to be home for at least another half hour. After debating whether to sit on the sidewalk and wait for him, I decided to press onward.

It was the longest 200 yard walk of my life. Barely able to lift my legs, I climbed the steps and stumbled into the house. I didn't know if I'd recovered from a virus to catch the flu, or what was going on.

While browsing online for Coronavirus symptoms, I watched videos, read reports, and learned the virus frequently kept people sick for a couple of weeks, went dormant for a week, then returned. Maybe my friends were right. Maybe I did have it, but I never felt warm enough to dig out the thermometer. Having been assured by the rude lady that COVID-19 was only the cough, an extremely high fever, and shortness of breath, I obviously couldn't have it. Anyway, the shortness of breath was only occasional for me.

Many people lost their senses of taste and smell when they had the virus. Although I did not, my nose went into sporadic overdrive for the next year. Beautiful fragrances turned into strong nasty smells. Ugly odors were enough to throw people and shoes out of the house. Sometimes meals tasted rotten, like the meat or vegetables had gone bad.

All the talk about Coronavirus caused us to wonder about one of our writer friends who had been in and out of multiple hospitals in November and December. They couldn't seem to diagnose his problem. I will never forget him telling me how hard it was to breathe. He had other symptoms, too, but always tested negative for the flu. By early January, they decided he had some kind of strange lung cancer. In a week or two, I was attending his funeral.

Also before the virus supposedly hit Oklahoma, one of our sons was extremely ill and went to the Emergency Room, but they could not diagnose him either. They tested for the flu and strep throat. When the tests came back negative, they sent him home with a high fever and severe cough. We worried he might not survive, but he did.

About the time I felt well, they were shutting down America, except for essential jobs. Schools shut down for the rest of the year, nursing homes restricted access, libraries closed, many restaurants shifted to pick-up, take-out, or delivery, and the senior center turned us away.

A local restaurant had a glass room we could use for our writing critique groups. I always went in early and washed down the tables with a sanitizer spray. Any extra protection I could offer my senior citizen writer group was important. Each of us sat at a separate table for social distancing, but nobody wore masks.

Before long, I learned one of my younger cousins, who still had a couple of children living at home, had taken her life. Her mother said the stress and fear-mongering over the killer virus had literally scared her to death. She overdosed.

One of our writing group members lived in an assisted living home. Her husband died in the spring, but she hung on strong. Due to living in the main building, she was held prisoner, like everyone else, until they allowed the senior citizens access to the rest of the world, months later. We sure did miss her. She visited her family around Independence Day, and had to quarantine inside her small apartment for two weeks after returning home.

That summer, my aunt, the mother of the cousin who took her own life, came down sick. While going through cancer treatments, her health took a sudden downward turn, and she told her family she was dying. Her oldest son came to

Oklahoma to help her out. When one of her brothers died and she didn't call me, I wondered if she was okay. She had always been my family information source. So, I called to check on her. Nobody answered for days. Finally, I left a message that if she was mad at me, just say so, but please let me know she was okay. She called back and said she couldn't hardly breathe to talk, so she had not been answering the phone. A lot of the family had tried to reach her. I contacted them to explain why she had not returned their calls. A few days later, I lost my aunt.

In early 2020, my critique group friend in the assisted living center, secured an appointment for her first COVID-19 shot on the 21st of the month. Finally! But a couple of days before her appointment, she tested positive for the virus. She did fine until the cough put her in the hospital.

Those were scary times. Every day or two, I'd text her to say we missed her and the group was praying for her. She finally contacted me and said she was feeling better. She was able to talk without coughing and was in therapy to regain her strength so she could go home. We talked a few times, then our communication halted. There was no mention of anything on her Facebook page, or any of her family's pages. When her phone line was disconnected, we knew she had died. Just like that. She'd had some other dangerous health issues, possibly caused by the virus, and they took her life.

We lost a lot of friends before the nation re-opened. Some died directly due to the virus. Some had residual stuff after the virus that finally took them. To me, they died from the virus. Why? If they had never had the virus, they probably would still be alive.

The numbers of infected people rose sharply around November to December of 2020, probably due to the holidays. So we didn't meet for a couple of months, then started back after many had been vaccinated.

Other than the writing group member who died before the virus was supposedly here, and the one who died after almost recovering, the rest are still with us.

Although my husband has had no lingering symptoms, I had "flashback" symptoms every month for nearly a year, as if the virus wanted to remind me how ill I'd been.

I'm pretty sure we did have COVID-19 in early 2020, because we wound up at the hospital for a whole day in February of 2021. COVID-19 patients sat all around us. One sat on the back of the seat I was in and one about four feet in front of me, both with fever. The virus was all over that waiting room. We all wore masks, but we also brought the germs home on our clothing, my purse, books, everything we had with us. We never had any symptoms or came down sick. I believe it was due to antibodies. And prayer. God is good.

Renee' La Viness has been published in newspapers, magazines and multiple short story and flash fiction anthologies. She climbed to the top of the career ladder as an editor at 4RV Publishing from 2013 - 2018. Currently, she edits short stories and children's books, sponsors and judges at least five annual writing contests, and serves as the advertising executive for Writers Monthly PDF eMagazine. Renee' has won more than thirty writing awards.

Into the Kingdom of Heaven

BY JONELLE GRACE LIPSCOMB

Grandmom brought Ladybird home the summer after I finished second grade. She said a woman had a box of puppies outside the grocery store that were "free" to a good home.

Earlier that summer, we had gotten a new dog, but not long after he came to live with us, he was hit by a car. Our house was right next to the highway and at the bottom of a steep hill. Cars would come speeding over the top and keep going fast all the way down. I found the dog when I went out to get the mail. I wasn't too sad because we hadn't had him very long.

We had another dog, Blackie, but he belonged to my brother Tommy, so I claimed Ladybird as mine. My grandad came up with the idea to name her after Lady Bird Johnson. I didn't really like President Lyndon B. Johnson because of the picture I saw of him holding his dog by the ears, but that wasn't really his wife's fault, and I did like the sound of her nickname.

Our Ladybird was small and short-haired, and she didn't have a tail. I had never had a dog without a tail. Grandmom said she was just a mutt, but when she got bigger, she looked a lot like the picture of the fox terrier in my book of dog breeds. Grandmom said we should start right away teaching her to stay in the yard and not follow Blackie, a male dog that liked to roam.

Ladybird loved people and always wanted to go with us when we went somewhere in the car. She would jump up and lie in the space above the backseat in the rear window. Sometimes on the way home from town, we stopped at the Dairy Queen for a treat. Grandmom gave me a nickel to buy an ice cream cone for Ladybird. I held the cone in my hand, and she licked it until it was smooth across the top and then ate the rest in two bites. Since we didn't know Ladybird's real birthday, we celebrated each year on the anniversary of the day Grandmom brought her home. I made her something special like a hamburger patty for supper followed by ice cream and cake. She didn't even mind wearing a party hat on her head, and I always bought her a present. We gave her presents at Christmas, too. In the winter when it was cold, she slept with me at night on my bed. When it was nice, though, she preferred to be outside. I didn't like the idea of her being outside with Blackie and tried tying her to my bed with the leash, but Grandmom said that wasn't fair to Ladybird.

In the summer, Ladybird and I went for long walks in the woods. We crossed the meadow to the other side where a creek ran down the side of a hill. Sometimes I took a picnic lunch. In the winter, Ladybird ran ahead of me in the snow leaving footprints for me to follow.

One year, my Aunt Nelle gave my brother and me each a baby chick for Easter – one boy banty and one girl. After they got big, there were baby chicks everywhere. The boy rooster was special. He strutted around the yard, fluffing his blue, red, and purple tail feathers—cocking his head from side to side—blinking his eyes. One day, the screen door on the side porch was propped open, and he wandered inside. We kept an eye on him in case he had an accident, but he didn't. He merely pecked up crumbs he found on the floor.

Every now and then, we invited him back inside. We named him Mr. Elvin. I'm sure there was a reason we named him that, but I don't remember. He was the boss of all the chickens, and at night he flew to the roof of the side porch and the other chickens followed. Grandmom said they did that to keep safe from the chicken-killing wild animals that came out of the night shadows. The side porch was officially renamed the "chicken" porch. Despite their efforts to stay safe, one by one the chickens either died or disappeared until there was only Mr. Elvin left.

He must have been lonely because he started following Ladybird around the yard. Rather than putting Ladybird's dogfood in a bowl, each morning and night I emptied half a can onto a flat rock next to the porch. One evening while Ladybird was eating, Mr. Elvin walked right up to the rock. I stepped forward to shoo him away before Ladybird had time to get angry, but then she stepped aside to make room for Mr. Elvin. From then on, they shared the same meals and hung around together in the yard. Nobody ever believed me when I told them my dog's best friend was a chicken.

Aunt Nelle, who lived half a mile down the road, had an entire coop of chickens, which she kept mostly for eggs. One of the chickens was a little crippled hen. Aunt Nelle said the hen was being picked on and pecked by the other chickens.

"Do you think Mr. Elvin would be kind to the little hen?" she asked.

We decided it was worth a try. She was small, black with white speckles, and her legs didn't work right. She would stretch one foot out in front and then twist and jerk her body to get the other leg to go forward. For Mr. Elvin, it was love at first sight. He stayed right by her side and didn't seem to mind that it took her fifteen minutes to go three feet. He no longer had time for Ladybird.

About a week passed. I came out of the house and stopped abruptly, dropped the can of dogfood I was carrying, and screamed. Ladybird was standing over the body of the little hen, which she had just killed.

I guess chickens must have short memories because it took only a few days before Mr. Elvin and Ladybird were once again friends. They stayed friends until Mr. Elvin disappeared one day. I didn't like to think that a wild animal might have killed him. Instead, I decided that since he was getting old, he had gone off somewhere to die like dogs sometimes do. You could tell Ladybird missed him, but she still had me. We still went on walks, but by the time I was in seventh grade, I didn't make as big a deal of her birthday as I once had.

On Sunday mornings, I went to First Baptist Church with Grandmom. Tommy went to the Christian Science Church with Aunt Nelle, and Granddad usually stayed home. One Sunday, I finished getting dressed for church and hurried down to the car where Grandmom was waiting. We pulled out of our driveway onto the highway, and Grandmom hit the brakes. Ladybird, unmoving, lay in front of us on the road. My stomach turned to ice, and I screamed.

I felt Grandmom's hand on my arm. "Jonelle, I want you to go up to the house and wait for me."

I pulled away, threw open the door, and ran toward my dog. "No, no, no!" I cried and reached to touch her, but Grandmom rushed up beside me and pulled back my hand.

"No, no, please, God, no," I sobbed.

"Jonelle, go to the house."

"I can't leave her. She's hurt. We have to do something. Please do something."

"There's nothing we can do. Now go to the house while I take care of this," her voice was firm. "Go on."

I turned and fled. When I reached the house, I ran into the bathroom and shut both doors. My body shook. I paced like an animal in a cage. "Please, God, please bring Ladybird back to life. You raised Lazarus from the dead. You can do the same for her. Please, please, please, God. Please let her live."

I was still praying when Grandmom opened the door. "Did God bring her back to life? Did he save her?" I asked.

She stepped into the room. "No, Jonelle, God couldn't save her."

The sobs came again as she folded her arms around me and pulled me close.

My grandmother buried Ladybird in the pet cemetery beneath the tree in the field beside the house. Her grave was surrounded by the graves of the dogs, cat, and hamsters that had gone before her. I brought the cross I had made from two sticks joined together and placed it at the top of the small mound of earth. My grandfather and brother joined us, and I conducted the funeral service.

I didn't understand why God didn't save her when I believed that He could, but I still prayed that he would take her into the kingdom of heaven, even though she had killed the little crippled hen.

Jonelle Grace Lipscomb is a writer, photographer, director, actress, and educator. She holds degrees from both the University of Arkansas and the University of Georgia. She pursued a career in the arts before teaching drama and filmmaking at Fayetteville High School. Now retired, Jonelle primarily remains involved in writing and photography. Her short story "Visiting Mother" was included in the anthology Writing Our Lives Volume II, published in 2017 by Writing Our World Publishing, and "Tommy and Me" was included in Writing Our Lives Volume III, published in 2020. Her short story "Someday" as well as a photograph "Trees and Clouds" and the poem "I Have Loved You" were published in the Arkansan Review. Another photograph "Moon in Trees" was published in the University of Arkansas literary magazine Diamond Line. Several of her stories have either won or placed in writing contests. Jonelle is currently enrolled in the M.F.A. Creative Writing Program at University of Arkansas Monticello.

Where Did All The Bathroom Tissue Go?

BY ANGEL MORGAN

Where did all the bathroom tissue go?

So went the question in early 2020. It was a year like no other in recent times. The year started normally. Slogans for the year that would be 2020 rolled off people's tongues as clever as ever, like "perfect vision in 2020" and "seeing clearly in 2020."

However, 2020 brought to light something no one was expecting, a pandemic with the name COVID-19 because research found that this strain of the virus first appeared in 2019. So, while this military town in North Carolina prepared for an illuminous 2020, the COVID -19 virus detoured the idea. The year 2020 changed lives by testing our fortitude in relationships, our ability to love ourselves in solitude, and it shined a light on the dark parts of who we are as a society.

It all began at the end of February 2020 and continued through March 2020, when no one could find bathroom tissue, paper towels, Lysol, or disinfectant to purchase. As bathroom tissue flew off the shelves, there were reports of increased COVID-19 cases and deaths, hospitals filled with COVID-19 patients, and businesses closing due to increased cases of the virus.

As businesses closed and people social distanced themselves by remaining indoors, the outside world closed. Who would have thought our world would *close*?

This fostered a new way of existing and co-existing with others. The norm became social distancing, wearing gloves and masks, not being around or touching family members, washing hands for at least 20 seconds, using alcohol, and washing everything when coming in from outside. It was a scary and uncertain time.

Experiencing personal sorrow in the latter part of 2019, when I lost both my mother and my sister four days apart, I wanted nothing more than to be around family. However, the pandemic erected an invisible boundary and created space between my loved ones and me. I did not want space or solitude. I did not choose to be alone, and I longed for an embrace from family and friends.

Even in the workplace, there were noticeable changes. Coworkers wore masks while others wore gloves as well. Coworkers spoke to each other at the threshold of office doors, allowing for six feet or more of distance from each other. At the beginning of March 2020, it was business as usual, however,

By the middle of March, some coworkers were told to wear masks because maybe they came into contact with someone with "The COVID." These were the murmurs around the office. So called, "The COVID," "Coronavirus" or "Rona," as many African Americans referred to it, placing a quintessential spin on the term.

By the end of March, some of my coworkers and I were cleared to work remotely. Still, businesses shut down, schools closed, and children were schooled virtually from home. The term "essential worker" became a common phrase, as we all wondered if the outside was ever going to open up again.

The most illuminous of 2020 came during the social unrest, protests. and global awareness from the killing of George Floyd. The social justice movement impacted the world, shining a light on injustice. In the South, there were protests for days during the pandemic. Even though I was not actively at a protest, I was in support of the righteous indignation that protestors showed. I thought, *What courage must people have to risk their health and safety for justice during a global pandemic? What tenacity and resilience it takes to endure and continue to stand for what is right and just.*

The news of skyrocketing deaths and quarantining began to create a mental health crisis in which people developed increased anxiety, depression and worry. All of this, along with the killing of George Floyd, exacerbated and compounded these same symptoms for African Americans.

Living in a society where one's humanity is denied and one's existence marginalized, for me and certainly other African Americans, the mental exhaustion from living through this historical time was both invigorating and daunting. It was invigorating to witness the emergence of a movement that had not been seen since the Civil Rights era; yet it is daunting that the marginalization, systemic racism, and killing of African American people continue.

I watched the scenes of crowds coming together for social justice. It was remarkable, as were the people who placed their lives, their health, and their freedom in jeopardy for justice during this pandemic.

With all the tension and mental anguish in 2020, the isolation of the pandemic was dismaying. I did not see my family in person for months or touch another human being without gloves. I was ready to feel my loved one's hugs, to see their smiles. However, I reminded myself that we were in a pandemic and staying safe was paramount.

Forced to spend many hours with myself, I spent time in self-reflection and began to miss family even more. Thanks to Zoom, Facetime, social media, and movie platforms like Netflix and Netflix Party, we could connect virtually for a reprieve from the constant reminders of being in a pandemic. In addition, I was grateful for the many Zoom sessions and trivia games played with loved ones during this time.

In tune with the sadness and loneliness we were all experiencing due to COVID, a clever deejay came up with a brilliant idea: Club Quarantine. *Thank you, D-Nice, for this small but important gesture of playing music to stimulate our endorphins for brain happiness and lifted spirits.*

From people's homes, they could watch and listen to D-Nice play songs that lifted sadness and bought people together, virtually, for relief from the harshness of the COVID pandemic and the fight for equality and social justice.

As we move to COVID-19 vaccines for the masses and chase elusive herd immunity for others, we've learned that some in the African American community are still concerned about receiving these injections.

When things began looking brighter in spring 2021 with the continued wearing of masks, social distancing and the availability of vaccines, the outside finally began to open up. Sure, some things have not changed: there is still COVID-19, social inequality (even with the signing of the Juneteenth bill), sadness, anxiety and many other issues plaguing us as individuals and as a society.

I am uncertain about whether not wearing a mask is good for society. However, everyone has autonomy, and the choice to mask or not to mask belongs to each individual. For me, I continue to wear a mask. As this society returns to some sense of normalcy, I am thankful for life, health, family, friends, employment, and for being able to purchase the bathroom tissue that is no longer missing.

Angel Morgan resides in North Carolina. She holds a master's in Social Work and is a Clinical Therapist who enjoys reading, writing, Tai Chi, poetry, and community work. She teaches Tai Chi virtually and offers mindfulness relaxation techniques. Angel has facilitated and instructed classes for youth in poetry and writing at a music, writing and arts program in the Fayetteville, North Carolina area. She has also hosted multiple poetry and other events throughout North Carolina. In addition, Angel has a book of poetry that will be released by the end of the year, and she is in the process of writing additional memoirs. She can be reached at AngelMorganisme@gmail.com

Ned

BY PAULA RELEFORD

My mama never really admired anyone in her life except my daddy. She was always drilling into us just how very special he was. A look of love mixed with something that I will never be able to put into words leaped into her eyes whenever she spoke of him.

I can't actually remember his face but, in my imagination, I recall his face was quite handsome. Mama would tell us that my brother, Ned, had qualities so much like daddy's. Ned is the person I most admire. He is strong, courageous, and kind with that goodness from his soul that so many others lack. Often I wonder how he survived in the world that surrounded him. I look at his picture now, a little photo in black and white, and I can almost hear his graciousness, softness, and greatness. For all of his life, he would be destined to be looked upon as a nothing, no more than a pebble that was slipped upon, a void in humanity's constellation. Yet to those who loved him, he was hope and life. It's strange how a person's most vivid recollections can be related to tragedy. I recall well the day our lives were shattered, and my mama lost her laughter and stopped singing forever. There were five of us children; Ned,10; Anna, 6.; Angela, 3; Cora,1; and me, 7.

While Angela and little Cora napped; Anna and I were out back picking turnip greens for dinner. Those were Mama's favorites, and that day was her birthday. She was outside hanging up laundry when we heard a loud burst of laughter and squealing. I looked around and sure enough, there was Daddy whirling and twirling her around—kissing, hugging, and playing.

Anna and I watched this familiar display for quite some time. I remember the dancing in Mama's eyes, the pearly whiteness of her teeth as they flashed brilliantly, the joy radiating from her lovely face. To this day, we honestly don't know where she was born or who her folks were. She was a small woman, not much taller than Ned. Her skin was the color of rich cream dotted with freckles across her nose and cheeks. With her long, straight, strawberry blonde hair, Mama appeared Whiter than most actual White folks.

The man that was my daddy, on the other hand, had the complexion of a big chocolate bear, deep and rich with soft brown eyes. He was tall, lean, and strong. Ned took his body build from him. Daddy worked on the new railroads. This was a real honor for a Negro man in those days. Most poor people worked in the field or in slaughterhouses. He had worked from the time that he turned six-years-old. I guess that's why when he was seventeen riding the train, he saw my mama working in the bean field. He inquired about her, courted her, and paid forty-five dollars for permission to marry her. She was twelve-years-old when she became his wife. As we stood there gazing at the two of them, I felt all the love that they had for each other, and it radiated to the very core of my spirit. I knew that was just the way that they both felt about each of us.

The thing that would destroy us came so violently that, to this very day, it still seems like a nightmarish thought. The reality of it will never fully penetrate my mind because of its intensity and swiftness. There was no warning, no time to prepare or to even contemplate. As our young eyes beheld this vision of splendor before us, there came a terrible ruckus.

I heard them before I saw them. All of a sudden, the yard was filled with men on horses. Dust flew up so thick that it became impossible to see. We moved further back in an effort to hide. They were shouting and laughing and saying horrible things, all at the same time it seemed. M y daddy was beaten, and my mama's clothes were torn from her body. I could neither look away nor shield my eyes, or even move. This moment would be frozen in time for the rest of my life. Never again would I feel safe and secure in this world.

When the attack was over, the men simply got back on their horses and rode off. My daddy lay bleeding, broken . . . and dead on the ground. Mama was only half conscious. She was face down in the dirt, torn and battered. Anna stood there beside me, her eyes wide and glassy. Her mouth had stretched over her face as if she would scream. That scream or any other sound stayed buried within forever. She was now suspended in time, in a moment where her only reaction was to urinate down her legs. The air around me grew cold even though it was mid-July. Everything looked dark and ominous. Fear overshadowed all that was good and lifelike. I felt myself age beyond my years. My very soul's substance dissolved into nothing more than pure pain. At only seven-years-old, I had already witnessed this thing—tragedy—and there would be no forgetting it . . . ever.

I stumbled out into the yard. Mama was still struggling. She didn't resemble the person that I knew. Her face was so different, grotesque, and discolored. My hands refused to touch her as she stared past me.

I moved out to Daddy now, where horror of such magnitude awaited. Even now I couldn't possibly describe it fully. The face that, just this morning, had been my daddy was now a complete mass of red and white fluid. In truth there was no face at all. Just mush. That's all. Then came a void, the null phase of mind. For at that second, true darkness overtook me, and my world faded out to nothingness.

Paula Releford is a resident of Fort Smith, Arkansas. She has three children, six grandchildren, and three great-grandchildren. Paula enjoys reading, gardening, storytelling and cooking. Her favorite form of writing is active fiction.

Under the Mattress

BY JOSEPHINE RUMPH

Carl offered me the rolled-up paper containing marijuana. I'd never held anything that sinister in my hand before—except maybe the girly magazine I discovered under my brother's mattress. But this. This was my first opportunity to be bold and bad. So, I took it and embraced the notion that he thought I was worthy enough to share his stash.

"Fire it up when you get home. It'll help you relax."

He took a pack of cigarettes from his inside jacket pocket, tapped it a couple times on the palm of his hand to allow one to escape. He placed the cigarette between his lips, lit it, and breathed in deeply. I sat on the passenger side of the car with my feet planted on the ground. I watched him as he allowed the smoke to escape his mouth and mingle with the crisp, fall air. Even though the smell of the smoke caused my nostrils to ache, I wasn't about to tell him. I turned my head and stared toward the moon-lit skies to avoid the next installment of smoke he would let out.

"Girl, give me my blunt back. You ain't gonna smoke it. You probably hadn't seen one before."

There was *some* truth to his claim. And if I'd seen one, I would've assumed it was filled with tobacco. I'd seen my best friend's father roll tobacco in papers and smoke it. But this wasn't the same thing. This was illegal. Cool. Scary. This was everything that I wasn't.

"Carl, you don't know me. I know exactly what this is." I wanted to sound cool. Plus, I figured my intellect would outpace his smokey brain. I was a college sophomore. I assumed he worked at one of the industrial plants in the county.

"That's some good stuff. You better not let it go to waste. You gonna smoke it tonight?" he questioned as an afterthought.

"No, I doubt it. I just can't light it up when I get home," I turned my head again to avoid another round of his smoke.

"Ah now, don't waste my stuff," he lowered his voice to a whisper. "Give me my joint back. That's the best stuff around." He surveyed the parking lot to see if any of the church folks were within earshot. "You can't even stand a little smoke from a menthol. How you gonna do anything with a blunt?"

He was right; I'd stifled my need to cough several times.

"Don't worry about me. I can handle mine." I had no idea what that meant in the street lingo. I'd heard my older brother say it a few times and figured it would work as a quick comeback.

"I tell you what," Carl said. "Hide it under your mattress until you get ready to light it up."

Carl might have said more, but he was interrupted by one of the guys in his quartet, "Hey, Carl, c'mon help with the equipment. I got to get home. I got to be at work in the morning."

He stood the standard ten feet away. It was how the fellas operated when they weren't sure if the group member was in a "private" conversation. I never knew his name. He was certainly less popular than Carl, and he lacked swagger.

"Oh, ok, Man, I'm coming," Carl said and took a final draw from the cigarette before he dropped it on the ground, stepped on it, and twisted his foot to make sure he extinguished it.

"Alright girl," smoke escaped his mouth again. "Don't let my stuff go to waste. Make sure you hide it under your mattress," he admonished and walked off. "See you later."

"Is the program over?" Carl questioned as he approached his friend.

"Yeah, it just ended."

Their conversation faded as the chatter from people exiting the church grew louder. Now the once crisp air was filled with cheap perfume mingled with sweat and musk. This was worse than the scent of cigarette smoke Carl left behind. This was Saturday night at church. Correction. This was *every* Saturday night at church. With one exception, I'd never been given a blunt before. Nor had I ever had a conversation with Carl that left me *intrigued.*

After sitting on a hard pew for more than three hours, I'd left the sanctuary for fresh air rather than suffer through at least thirty more minutes of muggy ceiling fan air. I made my way to the car to sit, breathe, and wait for the program to end, or my sister to be smart enough to join me.

Carl finding his way to me was a fluke. I just happened to be sitting in the car, and he was obviously in need of some conversation for a few minutes. Carl never really came into the church to sit. His group was local celebrities. Most of his band members spent their time on the outside, talking with the other singers, the girls, or in the fellowship hall eating chicken or fish sandwiches.

Carl was a cliché: tall, dark, and handsome. He was second tenor and always took center stage with the quartet. His voice, powerful, sultry, and sexy, could set your soul on fire if you dared get caught up with his obvious sex appeal, rather than the ministry. I'm not sure if it qualified officially as a ministry. His quartet seemed to put on a show—although there was an undeniable authenticity in their effort. Whatever the case, every time they sang, folks would dance in the aisles as if they were filled with the Holy Spirit. The quartet did a variation of the same show. The musicians were modern-day hype men, who ushered the vocalists to the front of the sanctuary with an upbeat set, and the singers never disappointed when they stepped to the microphone. They entertained—or ministered to—the congregants with an up-tempo introductory song. After which they slowed the tempo to praise and worship. Finally, they closed their three-song set with the crowd's favorite. Everyone in attendance likely knew the routine but enjoyed it, nevertheless.

Whenever they finished their last song, the vocalists made a grand exit and left the crowd begging for an encore. Sometimes they would oblige.

Carl and I were from the same rural county, and we embarked on the same passion—love for gospel music. He loved to sing it. I loved to listen to it. That was our only commonality. It was nice to chat with him. His conversation was clean, not flirty, and anecdotal. It was strange my only takeaway was a marijuana thingy. I can't recall what led him to give it to me in the first place.

Holding an illegal substance in my hand overwhelmed me. Still, I examined it as if it were a thing of value. I didn't even have sense enough to put it away. Folks passed by, offered good-night wishes, and "How's your momma 'em doing?" to me. Still, I made no attempt to hide Carl's offering. I merely sat there, admiring my tiny piece of trouble. I felt nervously grown. Maybe the nervousness was guilt—*why was I drawn to this thing?*

By the time my sister finally made her way to the car, only a few people remained in the parking lot. She was in the company of her boyfriend, Roy, the base guitarist— the obvious reason for her delay. He was really smitten with her, and she enjoyed his company. He clung to her every chance he got.

"Hey, Phine, Carl wasn't over here giving you a hard time, was he?" Roy quizzed.

I laughed, "Why do you ask, Roy?" I was shocked he knew Carl and I'd been chatting.

"Because Carl's crazy!"

I didn't know if I should come clean about the weed. I didn't want to snitch on Carl. I noticed him walking toward us, so I avoided Roy's question in favor of whatever Carl would say.

"Hey man, Willie told me to come get you. We got to go," Carl addressed Roy as he made his way closer. "Did she tell you I gave her a joint?" Carl just blurted out without warning.

Roy grinned mischievously. "What chu gonna do with it, Phine?"

Carl didn't give me an opportunity to answer. "I told her to hide it under her mattress until she's ready to fire it up."

"See Carl, you shouldn't tell my business." I honestly had no idea what I was going to do with it. Hiding it under the mattress seemed like the only reasonable thing to do.

"Y'all better get in the van before you need to fire up your feet and walk home," the driver said as he slowly moved the group's van toward us.

"Dang, that's Willie driving. He may leave us out here in the woods. I'll see you next weekend, Baby," Roy kissed my sister on the cheek and trotted toward the van.

"Under the mattress" was Carl's final instructions. He made his way to the van, dropped his cigarette, and squashed it under his feet before getting inside.

"Carl gave you marijuana?" May Nell questioned.

"Yep," I opened my hand to expose it. A bona fide inquisition was sure to follow.

"What are you going to do with it? I know you don't plan to smoke it, do you?"

"I don't know. I haven't decided."

"Girl, you better throw that mess out the window."

"Naw, I'm keeping it. Besides it's no big deal, and I'm sure Roy smokes weed too." That should shut her up, I thought. But it didn't.

"You think Roy does drugs?" she asked.

"Yep, all of the musicians probably do," I chuckled. "You know none of them are real Christians. They never *really* come in the church and sit down. They just stand at the door and watch."

We arrived home around midnight. I made a beeline to the bedroom to put my illegal gain under my mattress. Before I left the room, I felt under the mattress to make sure it was secure. I took a quick shower thinking obsessively about the weed and whether it had somehow fallen onto the floor. As soon as I returned to the bedroom, I lifted the mattress to check. It was there. I pushed it closer toward the center.

I lay in bed thinking about the weed. *Should I smoke it? How do I smoke it?*

I thought about how Carl took a deep sucking breath, then blew out smoke. I tried to imitate him but choked on my spit.

How was I going to smoke when I couldn't even pretend to smoke?

It was silly of me to take the marijuana in the first place. I was fixated on the speck of mystery under my mattress.

The next evening, I had to return to college. My entire day was spent trying to figure out what to do with the weed. It was too risky to take to my dorm, so I left it under the mattress. I thought about it less and less as the days, weeks, and months passed. Two years later, I graduated from college and moved from rural Alabama to Little Rock, Arkansas. The marijuana was left under the mattress.

Carl became a born-again Christian. Ironically, the last time I saw him, he sang a solo at a special event in my honor. His voice was still powerful, but he had changed. He sang to God, a sweet, melodious, worship song. He didn't stand in the doorway and watch but sat with his wife during the entire event.

As I listened to Carl sing that evening, I thought about my *one* strange encounter with him twelve years earlier and wondered if he remembered the weed and his instructions. I hoped not. That was the old Carl. This was a new and improved version.

I suppose the weed rotted under the mattress.

And, unfortunately, Carl died from complications of COVID-19 in 2020.

JoSephine Rumph earned her BA degree in journalism with minors in English and criminal justice from Troy University, Troy, Alabama. JoSephine has written and produced several inspirational plays and skits. She recently completed her first novel, Broken Soul, set to be released in late 2021. JoSephine is a native of Barbour County, Alabama, and currently resides in Vestavia Hills, Alabama. JoSephine worked for several years at the historic Arkansas State Press newspaper. She later worked for the state of Arkansas in Little Rock. She went on to explore a career as a political consultant and helped several candidates win in key races. While JoSephine is a self-defined political junkie, she admits her first love is creative writing. JoSephine is looking forward to publishing a book of short stories with her teenaged daughters.

I Am the Son of the Nile

(AN EXCERPT FROM THE MEMOIR *I AM THE SON OF THE NILE*)

BY TEDDY WARRIA

I am the tenth of seventeen children from a polygamous Eastern African family. I was born at the 120 year-old Kenyatta National Hospital (KNH), which is the largest referral and research hospital in East and Central Africa. The original name of the hospital was the Native Civil Hospital, and the name was changed to King George VI in 1952. At birth, I was greeted with five ululations for being born as a boy-child with my mother's colleagues at the hospital joining in celebration. If I had been a girl-child, I would have been greeted with four ululations. The Luo community that I belong to puts a premium on the boy-child.

My aunt, Margaret Adhiambo Abong'o, and my mother's cousin, Connie, came bearing gifts and messages of goodwill to welcome my mother's second-born son, and my father's tenth born child. I was taken home to Buruburu I Estate, House No. 150, the crown jewel of housing estates in

Nairobi's Eastlands. This was my first home, and it gave me the foundation to flow like the river Nile to more than eighty countries within forty years of my life.

My father was a veritable symbol of unity; he embodied it. Our house was a household of a total of twenty-two people: seventeen children, one house helper, three co-wives, and my strong, able, and devoted father, *wuonwa,* George Edward Warria.

Sometimes there could be more visitors depending on the house guests from upcountry in Kisumu, which was about 224 miles from Nairobi, in the Lake Victoria region where my father was born in my home village of Kamnua, and my mother in her home village of Pith Kochiel in Seme—the home of the awe-inspiring Kit Mikayi, Ndere Island National Park, and Lupita Nyong'o, winner of an Oscar for *Twelve Years a Slave,* actor in *Queen of Katwe,* and author of the children's book, *Sulwe*, which means a star in Dholuo, my native language.

My parents were in the first wave of Africans to go to live and work in the capital city of Nairobi, after Kenya's independence in 1963 from the British colonial government run by Her Majesty the Queen Elizabeth II, who still reigns as the Head of the Commonwealth. My mother's paternal uncle, The Hon. Jonah Hezekiah Ougo Ochieng', then a Member of Parliament of Bondo—now Rarieda Constituency in Siaya County, where Barack Obama, Sr., hailed from—

arranged for my mother to come and join the nursing school at the Kenyatta National Hospital because he could. His brother was a medical doctor in charge of the leprosy research program at the hospital.

My mother started off well at the nursing school but became so afraid of seeing blood that she dropped out of the training. It is funny to think about this because much later in the US, my first job was as a phlebotomist, also known as a "vampire" since I used to draw blood from patients, which I was surprised the hospital referred to as clients.

I had a lot of fun drawing blood from the senior White American women in Lubbock, Texas, at the University Medical Centre (UMC). I had a habit of packing a lot of Hershey Kisses®--tiny, cone-shaped chocolates wrapped in aluminum foil—to prevent them from melting in my lily white lab coat pockets. As soon as the patient sat down and I had wrapped a tourniquet around their elbows, I would look at them straight in the eyes and ask, "Would you like a kiss?"

The patient looked delighted but surprised, "A kiss for me?"

"Let me give you a gentle kiss," I would say naughtily.

The patient seemed shocked and afraid that a young, Black man had asked that. I would then proffer my hand and give them a Hershey Kiss chocolate and a gentle, inviting smile, assuring the patient that everything will be okay.

The patient would smile and relax.

"Are you absolutely comfortable before I proceed?" I would ask.

Then I asked them to open and close their hands, to help pump their blood, as I prepared to draw their blood. Sometimes that was with a butterfly for the ones with delicate skins, and on the posterior surface of their hands. For those with stronger veins, I used small syringes, which I imagined felt like the bite of a pestilential female Anopheles mosquito. So, I hummed a heartfelt and soothing tune to calm the patient's nerves. This procedure was to be repeated many times until mastered.

One of my most challenging tasks was to arrive to my early morning shifts during the winter, which began at 4 a.m. in wards 4 East and 4 West. This was during the SARS epidemic in 2001, and we had to be robed and hooded to protect ourselves from being infected by the virus. I particularly enjoyed the yellow hood and disinfected surgical shoes that made me feel like I was dressed for a moon landing.

By the time I reached the fourth floor, I was exhausted but derived a heroic moment when my eyes caught a motto by Quintus Horatius Flaccus, known in the English-speaking world as Horace, which simply read: "Carpe Diem—Seize the Day!"

I lifted and stretched my right hand, a firm grip on my phlebotomist box with all the medical supplies. I resolved to start my day and shift, which ended at 2 p.m. every Thursday, Friday, and Saturday, with everything in me. Sunday was reserved to attend the First Baptist Church in Levelland, Texas.

One of the craziest incidents happened when I was on the fourth floor. I worked on a tight schedule, and each patient had to have their blood drawn within five minutes. This included my knocking on the ward doors to be let into their individual rooms, waking them up, and preparing them for the sometimes unpleasant experience of having their blood drawn early in the morning before the routine medical tests that had to be conducted.

On this particular morning, the patient was not in her bed when I entered the room. After searching frantically for her, I found her smoking and balancing delicately on the windowsill, closed, I presumed, to make sure the smoke detectors in the wards did not sound. She was wearing only her underwear and a white sleeveless upper-body garment, a vest.

I was quite relieved to find her, of course, but seeing her on the windowsill made me think she was planning to commit suicide by jumping from the fourth floor.

"Howdy Ma'am," I greeted her.

She replied, "I am cool, just smoking a darn joint, Bro."

Offering her my hand and speaking as calmly as I could muster, I said, "Please come down so that I can draw your blood."

She obliged, and I was so relieved. When I got out of her room, I raised my hand and said out loud, "Carpe diem." This became my life's motto.

This was the first of many hilarious experiences for me as I visited forty-eight of the fifty states as a young pre-medical student in America. The highlight for me was meeting the man from Hope, Arkansas, and comparing which one of us was wearing the best cowboy boots. Given that mine were made by genuine cowboys from West Texas, I won. And, I had spurs on mine and the inscription: "Warria. A genuine African."

Back at my father's house in Buruburu, we had a beautiful garden with colorful and delightful flowers. I especially liked the deep red and green foliaged poinsettia, which would ooze with white milk when you cut or plucked the leaf and was widely used in Christmas floral displays against our white house—an orange brick-roofed bungalow with a bamboo perimeter fence.

The urban legend was that should you bleed a lot, this elixir of white milk from the poinsettia leaf would stop it immediately. My mother, Wilfrida Atieno Warria, was the go-to person for all manner of ailments and accidents that required first aid. In fact, our house was called The Highway. This was because the doors were always open. and there was intense activity from our house and the fifteen other houses in Mugumo Court of Buruburu I Estate, Eastlands. It was also a symbol of unity. Today, most members of my Court are immigrants residing in many different countries around the world.

Some of the most memorable times at home in Buruburu were during the mid-80s, when my second eldest brother, Dan Warria, visited from Zürich, Switzerland, where he was a student. I was fascinated by his sophistication. He listened to jazz and loved Tracy Chapman's songs. I remember singing out loud, "Fast Car," "Talkin' bout a Revolution," "Baby, Can I Hold You," and "All That You Have Is Your Soul."

My brother also came with a sleek portable FM/AM Multiband Receiver Sony radio that he tuned to BBC World Service. A student at Rüschlikon University, he always transported me to different worlds with my imagination, my traveling mind. My brother always brought me brown, fine, dark brown and white milk Swiss chocolate since he also worked part-time at a chocolate factory. He also introduced me to youth-inspired and bright-colored Swiss Swatch watches and later to the elegant Mondaine Official Swiss Railways Evo2 Automatic men's watch, made of stainless steel and sapphire crystal to round out my timeless wardrobe. I learned to keep time. I learned a lot from him.

Those days, deodorants were not a norm in my country, and my brother had pleasantly scented roll-ons. In fact, he asked me if he could go and buy me some, and I obliged out of curiosity. When my brother visited during the summers with suitcases of gifts for all twenty-two of us, we all knew it was time to have mayonnaise, Tabasco® sauce, and cheese.

On one such visit when I was in the eighth grade, he took me and my sister, Ajwang' R. Warria, to the finest Italian restaurant in Nairobi called Trattoria, where we enjoyed Mama Russo's Mediterranean cuisine. My brother, being a little naughty, bought us a tot of Sambuca. Sambuca is an Italian, anise-flavored, usually colorless, liqueur. The vapor of the drink wafted through my nostrils, but the Sambuca burned my chest when I drank a shot. Just a shot. One shot. This, we never told our parents.

Dan also enjoyed taking us for the long trip to our home village of Kamnua in Western Kenya. My brother loved racing cars. He must have thought he was on the German Autobahn racing a Mercedes. We always stopped at the breath-taking resort, Kericho Tea Hotel, aptly described as the "hotel with the air of a country club," which served well-brewed tea with milk and sugar with an African-Indian pastry with meat known as a samosa or *sambusa* in Swahili.

The highlight was when my brother allowed us to roam in the tea farm and catch the verdant carpet view of black Kenyan tea before we continued with our journey for another two hours. When we arrived home in the picturesque Nyabondo plateau where Kamnua village is, my grandmother, Nina, would meet us at her gate, *rangach*, dancing and ululating, "*Alilililí*!" She continued dancing around us by shaking her shoulders until they appeared to come off their sockets. The dance is called *Goyo Otenga* in my native Dholuo language. My grandmother was a delight to behold and experience. An encounter.

Grandmother Nina would then lead me to her house, *odwa*, which means our house, because in our culture she was my "wife" too. She would call me her "husband" and ask me what I would like to eat. I was her husband in the sense that as a grandchild I was given and had the responsibility to carry my paternal grandfather's name, and she taught me how I should treat and maintain my future wife. I loved this tradition and custom.

After lovingly calling me by her husband's name, Warria, she would ask me to join her in her kitchen. I loved being in the kitchen, *kartedo*, of my late and beloved grandmother,

Mama Rosalina "Nina" Ajwang' Warria *Nyamawego*, whom my younger sister is named after. Grandmother Nina's kitchen was a sacred place for storytelling. She regaled me with folktales that were full of life lessons and local heroic deeds, sometimes exaggerated for effect, suspense, and humor. As my grandmother animatedly regaled us with these tales, our imagination fired up and connected with the distant past happenings, notably the Samson-like story of the revered Luo Warrior, Lwanda Magere of the Sidho Clan in Kano, Kisumu City County—the Lake City in the Sun, where the sun kisses the Equator 365 days a year. I fondly call it *KIS(S)UMU,* The Lake City of 1000 sun kisses.

These stories were often told to my siblings and me after sunset in the *kartedo,* around a three-stone fireplace, in a dimly-lit room, lit with a tin lamp (*tach nyangile),* with soup boiling on the earthen pot (*agulu*), in her grass-thatched rondavel kitchen that was outside her main house as the first wife, *Mikayi*.

Grandmother was the first of my grandfather Gordon Aoko Warria's eight wives. My kid brother is named after her husband.

Our grandmothers revered as the seat of wisdom were like an African leadership institution that was dismantled in the 21st century. I have long believed that reigniting this connection with our roots and heritage must be supported and institutionalized as we seek to be contributors and representatives of the new African narratives, as we regain our seat in a COVID-19 world.

This has become my new cause as I remember, honor, and amplify what my grandmother taught me and share it with the rest of the world, including my beloved southern United States, where West Texas was my home. The eyes of

Texas are upon me, wherever I go as a son of the Nile. Flow river flow, for I am wading in the water without splashing.

Teddy Warria (Kenya) is the author of Son of the Nile. He is an African entrepreneur and youth advocate. He co-owns Africa's Talking Group Ltd. and Focus Mobile Ltd. He supports access to educational opportunity for young minds worldwide. He is a Director of Climate Advocates Voces Unidas (CAVU.ORG). He is a champion for Africa 2.0, a pan-African civil society organization working towards an inspiring and prosperous Africa.

You are invited to attend the Read.Write.Share Writers Weekend 5th Annual Conference in 2022. Visit our website (https://www.rwsweekend.org/www.readwriteshare.org) where more information including specific dates(s), location, and agenda will be posted as soon as plans are finalized. (Note: Due to covid-19 the conference may be virtual again.)